Ch

D0351704

better spelling

Chambers

CHAMBERS
An imprint of Chambers Harrap Publishers Ltd
7 Hopetoun Crescent
Edinburgh EH7 4AY

First published by Chambers Harrap Publishers Ltd 2007
© Chambers Harrap Publishers Ltd 2007

A CIP catalogue record for this book is available from the British
Library.

ISBN: 978 0550 10338 3

Designed and typeset by Chambers Harrap Publishers Ltd, Edinburgh
Printed and bound in Spain by GraphyCems

CONTRIBUTORS

Editor
Christina Gleeson

Series Editor
Ian Brookes

Editorial Assistance
Vicky Aldus
Sheila Ferguson

Additional Material
Arthur Harrison

Prepress Controllers
Nicolas Echallier
Becky Pickard

CONTENTS

Introduction

To many people, English spelling is frustratingly inconsistent and unpredictable, full of pitfalls and uncertainties. Over the decades, countless systems and programmes have been developed to help teachers guide pupils towards correct and confident spelling, and most of us will remember the days of having to learn our 'spellings' every week, and the dreaded 'spelling test'. And yet, in spite of all this effort in our formative years, for many of us there are still some words that will always create a sense of disquiet and uncertainty, because we still are unsure about how to spell them. Of course, the spelling of a word can always be checked using a good dictionary, or a computer spellchecker, but these do not explain why the word is spelt the way it is, nor do they help us to remember the correct spelling once it has been checked.

This guide book, *Better Spelling*, is for anyone who wants to be sure that their spelling is completely correct all of the time. It provides check-lists showing the correct spelling of words that are commonly misspelt or confused with each other, but also warnings about likely errors, memory aids to help remember correct spellings, and clear explanations of the rules of English spelling.

Chapter 1 gives a simple but comprehensive historical overview of the development of the English language since the 5th century AD, explaining how the language has evolved over the centuries and how a variety of influences, including invasions from foreign nations, and social, political and cultural factors, have shaped the language to make it what it is today, helping to explain why, unlike many other languages, its spelling is so apparently unpredictable and inconsistent.

INTRODUCTION

Chapter 2 provides a comprehensive list of the main spelling rules of English. The rules are listed in alphabetical order according to the topic covered, for example **-ance, -ence** (where the rules on spelling words like *appearance*, *preference* and *occurrence* are explained). This chapter also gives some useful spelling tips to help you learn and remember the more difficult spellings, together with warnings about exceptions to the rules and common mistakes. There are also information panels which present interesting and useful information about the language as an additional aid to good spelling.

Chapter 3 lists the most frequently misspelt words in English, pinpointing where mistakes are likely to be made and often providing a spelling tip as a memory aid to help you remember the correct spelling in future. Another important feature in this chapter is the use of cross references (marked ▶) to relevant spelling rules in Chapter 2, which will help you relate the correct spelling of a word to a general spelling rule.

Chapter 4 lists words that are similar in sound and/or spelling and are therefore sometimes misspelt or confused with each other. The differences between the words are clearly indicated by explanations and example sentences, and again memory aids and cross references to general spelling rules have been inserted where appropriate to help you remember the distinctions between the words once you have grasped them.

Chapter 5 shows how understanding prefixes and suffixes can be a useful aid to good spelling. Prefixes and suffixes are groups of letters added to words or roots of words to create new words. (A root word stands on its own as a word but can be added to.) For example, knowing that the prefix *hydro-* means 'water' will help you spell words like *hydroelectricity*, *hydroponics* and *hydrofoil*. This chapter explains how prefixes and suffixes are used as combining elements in English to build new words and extend the meanings of existing words, and lists the most common prefixes and suffixes, together with their meanings.

Although the emphasis throughout this book is on British English, the differences between British and American usage and spelling have been highlighted in various sections. In addition to this, you will find some general comments and a list of the most common differences between British and American spelling in Chapter 6.

Chapter 7 provides some tips for helping you improve your spelling. It is divided into three sections: specific techniques for learning difficult spellings; general spelling strategies; and ways of checking that you have spelt a word correctly. This chapter covers memory aids to help you remember a spelling, such as using mnemonics (a rhyme or guide that helps you to remember something), ways of analysing words to help you spell them correctly, such as looking for letter patterns in words, and methods for checking your spelling, such as tips on using spellcheckers and dictionaries.

The book also contains, in an appendix, a handy list of all the common spellings for vowel and consonant sounds in English so that, if you have searched for a word in a dictionary or word list and have not found it, the list will suggest other possible spellings of the word for you to search for. For example, if you have searched for *knapsack* in a dictionary under the letter *n* and have not found it, consulting the list will show you that there are four other possible spellings for words beginning with an *n* sound: *kn*, *gn*, *pn* and *mn*.

This guide to *Better Spelling* covers all the main aspects of English spelling and has been structured so that it can be read from chapter to chapter, thus enabling you to build up a gradual, deeper knowledge and understanding of the fundamentals of English spelling. However, the bulk of the book can also be used as a reference tool, to be dipped into whenever that feeling of uncertainty creeps in and those tricky spellings elude you.

1 Why are words spelt the way they are?

The difficulty with spelling

Look at these words. Can you say which are spelt correctly?

accomodation

comparitive

definately

embarassed

fourty

hygenic

independant

innoculate

necesary

questionaire

sattelite

seperate

In fact, they are all spelt incorrectly. The correct spellings are *accommodation*, *comparative*, *definitely*, *embarrassed*, *forty*, *hygienic*, *independent*, *inoculate*, *necessary*, *questionnaire*, *satellite* and *separate*.

These are all commonly used words, but they are frequently misspelt. Yet how many times have you ever stopped to think about them? Often the wrong spelling looks as though it *could* be right or even *should* be right. Even good spellers have blind spots with apparently easy words: when I make up a shopping list, the word 'carrot' never looks right to me. I want to add a second *t*, even though I know it shouldn't be there. A recent newspaper headline about the Sahara Desert used the word *dessicated* in large letters instead of *desiccated*. It must have looked correct to the writer and the subeditor. (I can only remember the correct spelling of this word by associating it with *coconuts* – both have two *c*'s and one *s*.)

Then there are those pairs of words which sound the same but have slightly different spellings: *council* and *counsel*, *discreet* and *discrete*, *principle* and *principal*. There are many such pairs in English where the sound of the word is no help to getting the correct spelling.

Yet the spelling of many European languages is almost entirely predictable. People writing Finnish, Estonian, Latvian, Lithuanian, Hungarian, Polish and other languages of Eastern Europe can expect to guess the correct spelling from a word's sound with almost 100 per cent confidence. Italian and Russian words can be guessed with a probability of about 95 per cent, Spanish words around 92 per cent, and German words around 90 per cent. French and Dutch are less predictable, but they do have rules which allow you to guess correctly most of the time. English, which offers less than 50 per cent predictability, sits firmly at the bottom of the league.

Why is English spelling so difficult? The purpose of an alphabet is, presumably, to represent the sounds of a language in a predictable way. Yet English often deviates from this principle, as we all know to our cost. In this chapter we will look at the discrepancy between sound and spelling and ask whether anything can be done about it.

Letters and sounds

When the Anglo-Saxons came to Britain in the 5th century AD, they used Runic symbols when they wanted to record inscriptions on bark. As Christianity took hold over the British Isles at the end of the following century, it adopted the 23 letters of the Latin alphabet, which were already familiar to the indigenous Romano-Celtic population. The letters *j*, *u* and *w* were added later to give us our 26 letters.

Of these 26 letters, three are now completely unnecessary for the purpose of indicating unique sounds. The letter *c* could be represented by *s* or *k*, *q* by *k*, and *x* by *ks* or *z*. But they each existed in the Latin alphabet, and so they became part of our spelling system.

A few of the letters are nearly always pronounced in the same way wherever they occur, and this can give us confidence when trying to read an unfamiliar word:

- The sound of the letter *v* is almost always the same, as in *van*, *save* and *avoid*.
- The sound of the letter *j* is almost always the same, as in *jam*, *judge* and *adjust*. (It has a different sound in a few words borrowed from other languages, such as *rioja*.)
- The sound of the letter *f* is almost always the same, as in *family*, *café* and *fudge*. The most notable exception is in the word *of*.
- The sound of the letter *z* is generally predictable, as in *zoo*, *quiz* and *gaze*, but it can also have other sounds, as in *pizza* and *seizure*.

Other letters are not so easy to guess. The letter *c* may be pronounced with an *s* sound, as in *city*, or with a *k* sound, as in *cat*. The letter *s* may be pronounced with an *s* sound, as in *sit*, or with a *z* sound, as in *rise*.

But the problem with spelling goes deeper. When we are reading, we can be confident about how to pronounce *j*, *v*, *f* and *z*, but knowing how a word sounds does not help us know how to spell it. There is only one way to pronounce the letter *j*, but the sound associated with that letter can be rendered in spelling in at least eight different ways. The following words all have this sound, yet each creates it using a different combination of letters:

jam

e*dg*e

a*dj*oin

*g*em

sug*g*est

hu*ge*

sol*di*er

sandwi*ch*

Similarly, the sound associated with the letter *k* can be produced using a range of letter combinations:

*k*ing

*c*at

a*cc*ount

ba*ck*

stoma*ch*

uni*qu*e

Vowel sounds

The spelling of 'short' vowel sounds, as in *pat*, *pet*, *pit* and *pot*, is reasonably predictable. However, the 'long' vowel sounds can be created by a wide range of letter combinations.

There are at least six possible spellings of the sound *ar*:

c*ar*

f*a*ther

cl*er*k

c*al*m

*au*nt

h*ear*t

Other 'long' vowels can be created in an even greater range of ways: there are at least eight different spellings for the *ur* sound, nine for the *oo* sound, and ten for the *aw* sound, but the gold medal goes to the *ee* sound, which has at least twelve possible spellings:

tr*ee*

l*ea*f

p*ie*ce

dec*ei*ve

*oe*strogen

an*ae*mia

k*ey*

qu*ay*

p*eo*ple

pol*i*ce

recip*e*

miser*y*

Not only can one sound be made from numerous different letter combinations, but the same letter combination can be pronounced in many different ways. The letter combination *-ough* can be pronounced in seven different ways:

- In *through* it rhymes with *boo*.
- In *cough* it rhymes with *off*.
- In *rough* it rhymes with *stuff*.
- In *though* it rhymes with *go*.
- In *plough* it rhymes with *cow*.
- In *thought* it sounds like *or*.
- In *thorough* it sounds like the *-er* of *water*.

Silent letters

Another situation where there is a discrepancy between sound and spelling is in the case of silent letters. When these occur in words, the written forms must be learnt from memory:

WHY ARE WORDS SPELT THE WAY THEY ARE?

- *b* is silent after *m* at the end of words such as *climb*, *lamb*, *plumb*, *thumb* and *tomb*, and before *t* in words such as *debt*, *doubt* and *subtle*.
- *d* is silent in words such as *sandwich*, *handkerchief* and *adjacent*.
- *g* is silent before *n* at the beginning of words such as *gnat*, *gnaw* and *gnome*, and at the end of words such as *feign*, *reign*, *sign* and *foreign*.
- *h* is silent at the beginning of words such as *hour*, *heir* and *honest*.
- *k* is silent at the beginning of words such as *know*, *knee*, *knock*, *knit* and *knuckle*.
- *l* is silent after *a* in words such as *calf*, *calm*, *half*, *talk* and *walk*.
- *n* is silent after *m* at the end of words such as *autumn*, *column*, *condemn*, *damn*, *hymn* and *solemn*.
- *p* is silent at the beginning of words such as *psychology*, *pterodactyl* and *pneumonia*, and in words such as *cupboard*, *excerpt*, *raspberry* and *receipt*.
- *r* can be silent after vowels in words such as *air*, *bird*, *butter*, *colour* and *doctor*.
- *t* is silent after *s* in words such as *listen*, *fasten*, *castle* and *Christmas*.
- *w* is silent before *r* in words such as *write* and *wrong*, and before *h* in words such as *who* and *whole*.

Word endings

A major source of confusion comes with the endings of words. There are some sounds, occurring commonly at the end of words, which can be spelt in many different ways:

- The final sound -shun is spelt differently in na**tion**, suspi**cion**, dimen**sion**, mi**ssion**, fa**shion**, comple**xion**, musi**cian** and crusta**cean**.
- The final sound -er is spelt differently in port**er**, doct**or**, gramm**ar**, col**our**, cent**re**, plasm**a**, amat**eur** and zeph**yr**.
- The final sound -shus is spelt differently in infec**tious**, atro**cious** and an**xious**.

- The final sound -*shal* is spelt differently in *essen**tial***, *finan**cial*** and *controver**sial***.

There are several other final sounds that present several spelling options, including the sound that could be represented by the spelling -*ant* or -*ent* and the sound that could be represented by the spelling -*able* or -*ible*.

Double consonants

Possibly the greatest single difficulty of English spelling is the problem of when to use double consonants. Consonants always sound the same whether they are single or double. In fact, there was a time when English had no double consonants; they were invented in the 15th century to indicate whether the vowel preceding them was 'long' or 'short'. The rule was that a single consonant came after a 'long' vowel and a double consonant after a 'short' vowel:

diner	*dinner*
tiny	*tinny*
later	*latter*
holy	*holly*

If this rule were applied consistently, there would be no problem, although we would have to write an awful lot of double consonants. Unfortunately, it isn't. Consider the following pairs of words where the stressed vowel is short, but the consonant is sometimes single and sometimes doubled:

habit	*rabbit*
robin	*bobbin*
panel	*channel*
very	*ferry*

According to the rule, *habit* should be spelt *habbit* and *robin* should be spelt *robbin*. As you can see, there are many inconsistencies with double consonants. Why do *questionnaire* and *legionnaire* have a double consonant while *millionaire* and *commissionaire* have a single *n*, in spite of the fact that all the words from which these are derived end in a single *n*? Why should *hazard* and *wizard* have only one *z*, while *blizzard* and *buzzard* have two? Why do *embarrass* and *barrage* have a double *r*, while *harass* and *garage* have only one? An interesting feature of the latter examples is that some people now pronounce the second of each pair with the stress on the last syllable: *har-**ass*** and *gar-**age***, as if subconsciously trying to conform to the double consonant principle.

Why is there a discrepancy between sound and spelling?

This brief look at the oddities of English spelling has identified four main problem areas:

- multiple spellings for most consonant and vowel sounds
- silent letters
- variable spellings for word endings that sound the same
- double consonants

To understand why there are these discrepancies between sound and spelling, we need to look at how the English language developed over many centuries.

A brief history of English

Languages are influenced by those around them, either through normal contact or as a result of conquest. Like birds, words do not recognize boundaries. This is one of the reasons why all languages change over time.

All except one of the European languages can be grouped into families. (The exception is Basque, whose origins and kinship remain a mystery.) German is a member of the 'Germanic' family of languages, along with its offshoots Dutch, Danish, Swedish and

Norwegian. Spanish, French, Italian, Portuguese and Romanian are members of the 'Romance' family, which all evolved from Latin. Russian and most Eastern European languages are part of the 'Balto-Slavonic' family. Other European languages, including Finnish and Hungarian, are members of the non-European 'Finno-Ugrian' (or 'Ural-Altaic') family.

But English is unique. Britain was the point in Europe where the great European language families, the Germanic and the Romance, collided and fused into one. The Anglo-Saxon that arrived in the 5th century was a Germanic language and had a fairly close correspondence between sound and letters when the Latin alphabet was adopted for its spelling. There were a few discrepancies: there was no letter in the Latin alphabet for two *th* sounds in *thin* and *this*, each of which had its own symbol in the Runic alphabet. But on the whole the sound of Anglo-Saxon could be expressed in the Latin alphabet as well as any other language at the time.

The influence of Old Norse

The first major influence on both spelling and grammar was that of Old Norse, which arrived during the Viking incursions and settlements in the 8th, 9th and 10th centuries. Norse was also a Germanic language. The words were mostly short, one-syllable words without double consonants, such as *cast*, *leg*, *rid* and *from*. The letter *k*, which existed in Latin but was rarely used, was widely used in Norse and was adopted by Anglo-Saxon for words before an initial *i* or *e* (as in *kill* and *keel*) and after *s* (as in *skin* and *skull*), while Anglo-Saxon words used the letter *c*. Already there were two spellings, *c* and *k*, for the same sound.

Germanic languages commonly used the opening letter combinations *kn-*, *gn-* and *wr-*. These occurred in both Anglo-Saxon and Norse. In time, the opening *k*, *g* and *w* sounds weakened and disappeared altogether in English pronunciation, although they continued to be pronounced in other Germanic languages.

WHY ARE WORDS SPELT THE WAY THEY ARE?

The influence of French

It was, however, the fusion of English with Norman French after the invasion of 1066 that caused the greatest divergence between spelling and sound. The Germanic and Romance families were very different, even though they were both part of the wider Indo-European group of languages. Moreover, French was more than just an influence on English; it became embedded into the fabric of the language.

French was the language of the court, of the ruling classes, of administration, and of law and the national institutions until the 14th century. Meanwhile, Latin held sway as the language of the Church. It is strange to think now that the early 'English' kings such as Richard the Lionheart didn't speak a word of English. English, with its Germanic structure and vocabulary, was the language of the common people. But from this trilingual state of affairs, it was English that ultimately absorbed both French and Latin. The speakers of English adopted French words and used them alongside English ones with the same meaning, thus greatly expanding the vocabulary and providing a range of nearly equivalent words which now allow us to express levels of meaning and fine distinctions.

Some examples of this can be seen in the table below:

French	English
county	*shire*
city	*town*
village	*hamlet*
mansion	*hall*
residence	*home*
chamber	*room*
reception	*welcome*
liberty	*freedom*
fraternity	*brotherhood*
charity	*love*
companion	*friend*

English words tended to be short, having only a few suffixes to add at the end of words, while French inherited many more suffixes from Latin (for example, -*able*, -*tion*, -*ity*, -*ance*). Moreover, these suffixes had variable spellings, often depending on the vowel in the root of the original Latin word (for example, -*ible*, -*cion*, -*ety*, -*ence*). French also had prefixes at the beginning of words (for example, *con*-, *sub*-, *ad*-) which would cause problems with double consonants.

English words were generally more down-to-earth, homely and simple; French and Latin words were grander, more refined, more formal and remote. French pronunciation differed greatly from English. It was more nasal and each syllable had an even stress, while English had few nasal sounds and each word had one strongly stressed syllable. French had fewer glide vowels – additional sounds put in to ease the transition from one sound to the next – and it was here that the roots of many spelling problems lay. On the whole, the original spellings of French words were retained, but by the time English finally became the official language of the court, administration and the legal system, and every official document had to be written in English, our pronunciation had moved on. The grammar too had become much simpler; the inflected endings that had characterized Anglo-Saxon had largely disappeared.

The classical influence

A revival of classical scholarship in the 15th century meant that vast numbers of Latin and Greek words entered the language. The influence of Greek can be seen behind some difficulties of contemporary English spelling. Here are just some examples:

- The Greek letter *psi* is preserved in English as the combination *ps*. English kept the spelling according to the name of the Greek letter, but the *p* sound disappeared. Hence the spelling of words such as *psychology*.
- There is no letter for the *f* sound in the Greek alphabet, the nearest equivalent being the letter *phi*. This became *ph* when transliterated into English, so now all words with this sound that are derived from Greek are spelt with *ph*, as *telephone*, *phobia* and *photograph*.

- The Greek letter *chi* was pronounced rather like the *ch* sound in the Scottish word *loch*. This is not a natural sound in English and we tend to pronounce it with a simple *k* sound. But the *ch* spelling of its Greek name was retained for words derived from Greek: *character*, *chaos*, *chemistry*, and so on.

These few examples indicate how English remains respectful of the original spellings of words and does not alter spelling to conform to the natural speech patterns of English speakers.

The arrival of printing

Another significant development of the 15th century was the spreading of new knowledge and learning by means of printed books. William Caxton established the first printing press in England in 1476. From this point, the written form of words tended to become more fixed. It was just around this time that the pronunciation of the letters *gh* in words such as *night*, *eight* and *straight* was weakening to the point of disappearing altogether. We are now stuck with these *gh* spellings, although the sound has been silent for over five hundred years.

A few changes took place in spelling, such as the doubling of consonants to distinguish a preceding short vowel, the dropping of the letter *k* at the end of words like *musick* and *traffick*, and the dropping of the unnecessary *e* at the end of words like *shoppe* – it never was pronounced *shop-ee* as we sometimes like to think! However, there has never been a systematic reform of spelling. It has simply evolved.

Despite the arrival of printing, people wrote, if they were able to write at all, as they saw fit, often using different spellings of the same word within the same document. Fashion played a part, as did the prestige of prominent individuals.

By about 1600, there was a general acceptance that words should be spelt in a certain way, based on a possibly undue deference to the spelling forms used in classical languages. But there has never been a body set up to rule on matters of usage and spelling, and no planned reform to keep pace with language change.

The current situation

All alphabetic systems need to be reformed from time to time if they are to keep a close correspondence between letters and sounds. It may seem self-evident that an alphabet should represent sounds accurately and unambiguously, thus making literacy easier to achieve for everyone. However, the concept of universal literacy is a recent one. Throughout history, the ruling classes have sought to deny or at best limit access to the written word. The word meant knowledge and knowledge meant power. Until recently, it was never in the minds of the ruling classes to simplify our spelling to make it more accessible.

So we now have a system of spelling that is not systematic. It may sometimes be capable of explanation by reference to history, but it is certainly misleading as a way of reflecting the sounds of the contemporary spoken language.

Are there any rays of sunshine to dispel the gloom caused by our wayward orthography? Most certainly. One is the enormous vocabulary of English, greater by far than any other language, and the crowning glory is the simplicity and flexibility of the grammar.

The advantages of English grammar

Among the languages referred to earlier as having a close correspondence between sound and spelling, Russian and Lithuanian have extremely complicated grammars. Like Latin and Greek, they have different forms for words to denote different genders and a wide range of endings for nouns, adjectives and verbs, depending on their grammatical function. The English verb *play* has only four forms: *play*, *plays*, *playing* and *played*, but a regular Russian verb has 92 different possible endings. Other languages have fearsomely complicated word forms with a series of suffixes that create some very long words. French, Italian and German are considerably more complex than English, and only the Scandinavian languages come anywhere near English in terms of simplicity.

A few points will demonstrate the advantages of English:

- There is only one form for common words such as *the*, *my* and *your*. In other languages, you need a different form for masculine or feminine, singular or plural.
- You do not need to change the form of an adjective to make it agree with its noun. *Red* is always *red*, whether it refers to a boy or a girl, to one thing or to many things.
- English nouns have no 'case' endings to distinguish between the subject and object of the verb. Grammatical relationships are conveyed by the order of the words rather than the form of the words.
- There is no requirement to change a word according to whether it is a noun or verb. Many words can function as both.
- New words can be created easily by combining existing ones. You can see this process at work in recent words such as *make-over*, *downsize* and *outsource*.

What is the relevance of all this to spelling? Native speakers simply take their language for granted and are neither aware of the difficulties nor of the advantages, until they attempt to learn another language. The point is to illustrate that although spelling is undoubtedly and conspicuously a problem, it is more than compensated for by the advantages of a simple grammar. These positive features are a consequence of the same processes that have led to spelling problems. Simplicity, flexibility and range of expression have evolved with a price tag, but one that is worth paying.

What should be done about English spelling?

An obvious response to the discrepancy between sound and spelling is to reform the spelling system so that the letters correspond to the sounds. That would mean getting rid of double consonants, abolishing silent letters, and ensuring that each suffix had one agreed spelling and each vowel sound had one agreed symbol. If this were done, we would also get rid of *c*, *q* and *x*, which, as we have already seen, could all be expressed using other letters.

Although this idea might seem attractive, it does bring some problems. For example, when *s* is used to create a plural form, it is sometimes pronounced as an *s* sound (as in *cats*) and sometimes as a *z* sound (as in *dogs*). Do we use only the *s* in all cases, or should we sometimes change it to *z*?

Similarly, the letters -*ed* that are use to create a past tense have three different sounds, as in *landed*, *turned* and *jumped*. Do we really want three different endings, -*ed*, -*d* and -*t*, to show the past tense?

Another effect of making spelling match sounds would be that homophones (words that sound alike) would all have to be spelt alike as well. At the moment it is possible to discern between *so*, *sew* and *sow* in spelling, but that would not be possible in a completely phonetic system.

There are numerous other difficulties that would arise from a completely phonetic system. Perhaps the most pertinent is that no alphabet could ever cater for the wide range of accents and pronunciations used to speak English all over the world. A reformed spelling system would always be a compromise based on an agreed standard. At the present time, the closest thing we have to a standard is the English spoken in the south-east of England. This differs considerably from the 'Received Pronunciation' historically taught in the public schools and now often mocked as embodying the snobbishness of the upper classes. A reformed spelling system based on either form of English would have all of the problems outlined above, and there would be a further consequence.

English is international. A growing number of words, especially scientific and technical ones, would be unrecognizable if they were spelt phonetically. Their current spellings reflect their origins, and they would be torn away from their counterparts in other languages which, in their written forms, are often identical. Reform in a language that is confined to its national boundaries can be achieved, but English is not in that category. It no longer belongs to the English. It belongs to the world. It would be unthinkable to demand that the whole world must change the spelling of English, the foremost language of commerce, science and international relations, and the primary language of the Internet. We are two hundred years too late.

Changes will come from below, as they have always done. English will evolve in its own way and time. A form of writing that has evolved over centuries and has absorbed so many influences (albeit messily and whimsically), that represents the totality of the language from birth to maturity and that retains features of all the sources that have contributed to it is a good basis for a global language. Regularity is not necessarily what is required.

English has many advantages in other respects: a simple, flexible grammar, a wide vocabulary, a tolerance of many pronunciations and accents, and an inbuilt capacity for change and expansion. It would surely be foolhardy to tinker with one of its few genuine difficulties. So the answer to the question 'What should be done about English spelling' is this:

Master it, and leave it be.

2 Spelling rules

In this chapter we will explain some simple spelling rules, most of them to do with forming words from others. The information is set out in alphabetical order so that you can go straight to a particular point without having to read the whole chapter. As a starting point, you might find it useful to familiarize yourself with some of the vocabulary used in this guide to explain the spelling rules:

Vowels are the letters *a*, *e*, *i*, *o* and *u*. The letter *y* often performs the function of a vowel but is generally considered a consonant.

Consonants are the rest of the letters in the English alphabet.

A **syllable** is a part of a word that contains a single vowel sound and is pronounced as a single unit. For example, *dog* has one syllable, *swim|mer* has two syllables and *un|der|stand* has three syllables.

Stress is the emphasis put on a part of a word when it is spoken. For example, in *ambulance*, the part of the word that is stressed and usually spoken more loudly is *am-*.

A **prefix** is a set of letters at the beginning of a word that gives it a particular meaning. For example, *un-* at the beginning of a word usually means 'not', as in *unhappy*.

A **suffix** is a set of letters at the end of a word that gives it a particular meaning or that changes its part of speech. For example, *-ly* changes an adjective, like *slow*, to an adverb, *slowly*. A word may have more than one suffix: *help* + *-less* + *-ly*.

SPELLING RULES

What follows is not a complete list of spelling rules, and there are some exceptions to these rules (not all of which are shown). However, knowing these basic rules is a good starting point for being able to spell well.

-able, -ible

This pair of word endings causes problems for many people as there seems to be no logic as to which spelling to use. The problems have their roots in the rules of Latin grammar and unfortunately these rules do not apply to the grammar of English. However, there are a number of hints and clues you can memorize to help you choose the correct spelling.

Adding -able

If the core part of the word you want to spell is a complete English word in itself, then the correct spelling of the ending is usually *-able*:

accept → acceptable   break → breakable

detest → detestable   fashion → fashionable

lament → lamentable   pay → payable

remark → remarkable   respect → respectable

There are exceptions to this:

collapsible	deducible	reducible	convertible
contemptible	discernible	responsible	convincible

flexible	*sensible*	*forcible*	*resistible*

If the word you want to spell is connected with words ending in *-acity*, *-ality*, *-ate* or *-ation*, then *-able* will be the correct spelling:

capacity → *capable*   *separate* → *inseparable*

hospitality → *hospitable*   *application* → *applicable*

If the core part of the word you want to spell ends with a hard *c* (pronounced as a *k* sound), or a hard *g* (as in *dog*), the ending must be *-able*:

amicable   *implacable*   *navigable*   *delegable*

Spelling tips for -able words

If the word ends in a silent *-e*, drop the final *e* before adding *-able*:

advise → *advisable*   *debate* → *debatable*

However, if the word ends in two *e*'s, keep both when adding *-able*:

agree → *agreeable*   *foresee* → *foreseeable*

If the word ends in *-ce* or *-ge*, keep the *e* when adding *-able*:

notice → *noticeable*   *change* → *changeable*

There are a few other words that end in a silent *-e*, when the *e* may be kept when adding *-able*. These tend to be quite short words:

like → *likeable* or *likable*   *love* → *loveable* or *lovable*

size → *sizeable* or *sizable*   *blame* → *blameable* or *blamable*

If the word has only one syllable and ends in a single vowel followed by a single consonant, double the last letter before adding *-able*:

hit → *hittable*   *get* → *gettable*

If the word has two or more syllables and ends in a single vowel followed by a single consonant, whether or not you double the final letter depends on the pronunciation. If when you say the word you stress the final syllable, you should double the final letter before you add *-able*:

regret → *regrettable*   *forget* → *forgettable*

An exception to this rule happens with words ending in *-fer*. The final letter is not doubled:

prefer → *preferable*   *transfer* → *transferable*

With verbs that end in a consonant followed by *y*, change the *-y* ending to *i* when adding *-able*:

justify → *justifiable*   *vary* →*variable*

Adding -ible

If the core part of the word you want to spell is not a recognizable English word, then the correct spelling of the ending is likely to be *-ible*. There is, for example, no word *aud* in English, so *audible* is correct, not *audable*:

credible	*gullible*	*possible*	*legible*
fallible	*illegible*	*edible*	*visible*
ostensible	*incredible*	*compatible*	*eligible*

There are exceptions. A number of words you would expect by this rule to end in *-ible* in fact end in *-able*:

affable	*equitable*	*inexorable*	*palpable*
amenable	*formidable*	*inscrutable*	*probable*
arable	*indomitable*	*malleable*	*unconscionable*
culpable	*inevitable*	*memorable*	*vulnerable*

Words ending in *-ible* are often derived from a verb that has changed in some other way:

defend → *defensible*   *neglect* → *negligible*

permit → *permissible*   *comprehend* → *comprehensible*

There are some words to which you can add *-ion* to form a related word. The correct spelling of the ending of words formed in this way will almost always be *-ible*:

corrupt → *corruption* → *corruptible*

exhaust → *exhaustion* → *exhaustible*

A few words do not follow this rule:

collect → *collection* → *collectable* or *collectible*

correct → *correction* → *correctable* or *correctible*

detect → *detection* → *detectable* or *detectible*

predict → *prediction* → *predictable* (only)

> *Spelling Tip*
>
> Nouns formed from adjectives ending in *-able* and *-ible* will always end in *-ability* and *-ibility* respectively:
>
> *adaptable* → *adaptability*   *eligible* → *eligibility*
>
> Adverbs formed from adjectives ending in *-able* and *-ible* will always end in *-ably* and *-ibly* respectively:
>
> *presumable* → *presumably*   *responsible* → *responsibly*

Finally, there are many more words ending in *-able* than words ending in *-ible*. If, after applying all the tips and hints, you are still not sure how to spell the word, opt for the *-able* spelling.

-acy, -asy

Words ending in *-acy* and *-asy* are often misspelt, *s* being used when *c* is the correct spelling, and vice versa. The most common spelling by a long way is *-acy*:

accuracy	conspiracy	inaccuracy	obstinacy
autocracy	delicacy	intimacy	pharmacy

SPELLING RULES

bureaucracy	*democracy*	*intricacy*	*privacy*
celibacy	*diplomacy*	*meritocracy*	*supremacy*
confederacy	*fallacy*	*numeracy*	*theocracy*

> *Spelling Tip*
>
> Note that words ending in *-cracy* are related to words ending in *-crat* and that many of the other words ending in *-acy* are related to words ending in *-ate*.

There are a few words that end in *-asy*. The commonest are:

apostasy	*ecstasy*	*fantasy*	*idiosyncrasy*

⚠ **Warning:** Note the correct spelling of *hypocrisy*, which has no a in it. If you are in doubt, think of the related words, *hypocrite* and *hypocritical*.

Adjectives
See **-ed**
See **-er**
See **-y**

Adverbs
See **-ly**

-ae-, -e-
There are some words that you may see spelt with *-ae-* or just *-e-*. In British English the *-ae-* spelling is used, whereas in American English it is standard to spell the word with just the *-e-*:

aesthetic → *esthetic*	*haemoglobin* → *hemoglobin*
anaemia → *anemia*	*paediatric* → *pediatric*
anaesthesia → *anesthesia*	*encyclopaedia* → *encyclopedia*

The exceptions are *encyclopedia* and *medieval*, which are now more common than *encyclopaedia* and *mediaeval*.

al-
See **-ful**

-ance, -ence

Choosing between *a* and *e* when spelling words like *abundance* and *conference* causes difficulties for many, and there are few easy rules to help you make the right choice. However, there are some hints and clues which will help you spell these words correctly.

If the letter before the ending is a hard *c* (pronounced with a *k* sound) or a hard *g* (as in *dog*), the correct spelling will be *-ance*:

   arrogance   *elegance*   *significance*

If the letter is a soft *c* or *g* (pronounced with an *s* or *j* sound), the ending will almost always be *-ence*:

   adolescence   *intelligence*   *negligence*

⚠ **Warning:** Exceptions are *allegiance* and *vengeance*.

Look at how the endings of related words are spelt and this will give you a clue to which spelling to use. For example, if the word is related to a word that has an *a* in its ending, it will usually take the *-ance* spelling. If the related word has an *e* in its ending, the usual spelling will be *-ence*:

   dominate → *dominance*   *cohere* → *coherence*
   ignoramus → *ignorance*   *interfere* → *interference*
   tolerate → *tolerance*   *revere* → *reverence*
   vigilante → *vigilance*   *adhere* → *adherence*

⚠ **Warning:** Exceptions are *violence* (related to *violate*) and *perseverance* (related to *persevere*).

Nouns formed from verbs ending in *-ear*, *-ure* and *-y* end in *-ance*:

   appear → *appearance*

assure → *assurance*

ally → *alliance*

Nouns formed from verbs ending in *-r* can be spelt *-ance* or *-ence*, but there is a rule to help you make the right choice. If the final *r* of the verb is preceded by a stressed vowel, the ending will be *-ence*. If the stress is anywhere else in the verb, the ending will be *-ance*:

con**fer** → *conference*   **hin**der → *hindrance*

pre**fer** → *preference*   **ut**ter → *utterance*

> *Spelling Tip*
>
> These rules will apply equally to related words ending in *-ant/-ent* and *-ancy/-ency*. However, the following words are spelt *-ant* or *-ent* depending on whether they are nouns or adjectives:
>
> *dependant, descendant, pendant, propellant* (nouns)
>
> *dependent, descendent, pendent, propellent* (adjectives)

Note that when adding *-ance* or *-ence*, you may sometimes have to double letters, drop a final *e*, or change a *y* to *i*. For more information about rules for this, see **Doubling final consonants**, **-e** and **-y**.

ante-, anti-

Words beginning with *ante-* or *anti-* are sometimes confused because they are pronounced the same and have similar spellings. However, if you keep their meanings in mind, you won't go wrong.

ante- means 'before': *antecedent, antenatal, anteroom*

anti- means 'against' or 'opposite': *anti-aircraft, antibody, antisocial*

Words beginning with *ante-* are not hyphenated. Words beginning with *anti-* are usually only hyphenated if the letter following *anti-* is an *i* or a capital letter. There are exceptions – these will be shown in any good dictionary.

-ar
See **-er**

-ary, -ery, -ory
Words ending in *-ary*, *-ery* and *-ory* are often confused and unfortunately there are only a few general hints that can be given as a guide to their correct spelling. These are not rules, and there will be many exceptions, but the following points may help you make the right choices.

Firstly, words ending in *-ery* are almost all nouns. If the word you want to spell is not a noun, it almost certainly won't end in *-ery*. Compare *stationery* (noun) and *stationary* (adjective). The exception is the group of adjectives ending in *-y* that are based on words ending in *-er*:

> *blister* → *blistery*   *bluster* → *blustery*

Secondly, look at a related word and you should be able to spot the relevant vowel (*a*, *e*, or *o*) that will help you decide the correct ending.

> *burglar* → *burglary*   *secretarial* → *secretary*
>
> *deliver* → *delivery*   *baker* → *bakery*
>
> *director* → *directory*   *predator* → *predatory*

Often, the key vowel will be stressed in the related word:

> *imagination* → *imaginary*   *secretarial* → *secretary*

Thirdly, if the word is a noun and the letters that come before the ending do not make up a real English word, the ending is likely to be spelt *-ary* or *-ory*:

> *vocabulary* (there is no word *vocabul* in English)

laboratory (there is no word *laborat* in English)

Finally, if the word has a related *-ion* word, the ending is probably spelt with an *o*:

direction → *directory*   *satisfaction* → *satisfactory*

-asy
See **-acy**

-c
To preserve the hard *k* sound to words ending in *-c*, add a *k* before adding *-er*, *-ed*, *-ing* and *-y*:

panic → *panicked* → *panicking* → *panicky*

picnic → *picnicked* → *picnicking* → *picnicker*

⚠ **Warning:** The following words do not follow this rule and can be spelt in a variety of ways:

arc → *arcing/arcking* → *arced/arcked*

talc → *talcing/talcking* → *talced/talcked* → *talcky*

zinc → *zincing/zincking/zinking* → *zincy/zincky/zinky*

Note that no *k* is added when the final *c* becomes a soft sound (pronounced with a *sh* or *s* sound):

electric → *electricity*   *magic* → *magician*

-ce, -se
Some words, such as *license* and *licence*, are often confused in spelling. The correct spelling depends on whether you are using the word as noun or as a verb. In British English, the ending *-se* is used in verbs, and the ending *-ce* is used in nouns:

Use *-se* for verbs	**Use *-ce* for nouns**
to **practise** juggling	football **practice**
advised to keep quiet.	a piece of good **advice**

| to **devise** a test | a nuclear **device** |
| to **license** a drug | a driving **licence** |

> *Spelling Tip*
>
> It may help if you remember that *ice* is a noun.

Nouns relating to adjectives ending in *-ent* or *-ant* are spelt with *-ce* at the end:

different → *difference*   *ignorant* → *ignorance*

⚠️ **Warning:** In American English, *license* and *practise* are used for both the noun and the verb, and *defense*, *offense* and *pretense* are all spelt with an *s*. Also, the word for a tool used for holding objects is spelt *vise*.

-cede, -ceed, -sede

There are only three words that end in *-ceed*:

   exceed   proceed   succeed

And only one word that ends in *-sede*:
supersede

All the others with the same final sound end in *-cede*:

| accede | concede | recede |
| cede | intercede | secede |

-cion
See **-tion**

Doubling consonants within words

A common error is writing a single rather than double letter in words like *illegible*, *misspell*, *really* and *unnecessary*. If you consider how the words are formed, and how each part is spelt, you should be able to spell the word with confidence:

dissatisfaction	= *dis* (not)	+ *satisfaction*
illegible	= *il* (not)	+ *legible*
immortal	= *im* (not)	+ *mortal*
misspell	= *mis* (wrongly)	+ *spell*
really	= *real*	+ *ly*
suddenness	= *sudden*	+ *ness*
unnecessary	= *un* (not)	+ *necessary*

Doubling final consonants

Most English speakers know that the final consonant of many words is doubled when a suffix is added. The problem is that in many apparently similar words, the final consonant is *not* doubled when a suffix is added. Fortunately, there are rules governing when you should double a letter and when you shouldn't.

Firstly, if the suffix begins with a consonant, you will never need to double the final consonant of the word:

equip → *equipment*	*spot* → *spotless*
chief → *chiefly*	*kind* → *kindness*

If the suffix begins with a vowel, follow these guidelines.

Double the final consonant when adding a suffix if:
- the word ends in a single consonant
- the consonant is preceded by a single vowel sound written with a single letter
- the stress is on the final syllable (or there is only one syllable)

drum → *drumming*

omit → *omitted*

refer → *referral*

If any of the above conditions is not met, do not double the consonant:

melt → *melting*   (the word ends in two consonants)

dream → *dreaming*	(the vowel sound before the consonant is written with two letters *-ea-*)
enter → *entering*	(the stress is on the first, not the final, syllable)

Note that a *u* following a *q* counts as part of a consonant, so you would double the final consonant in the word *quit* since it is considered as being preceded by a single vowel.

Note also that even if a consonant is not pronounced, it usually still counts as a consonant for the purposes of the rule:

condemn → *condemning*   *calm* → *calmer*

A final *y* or *w* that is part of the written form of a vowel sound does not count as a consonant and is not doubled:

enjoy → *enjoyed*   *allow* → *allowed*

There are several exceptions to the rules for doubling final consonants:

1. A final *x* is not doubled – it is treated as two consonants since it is pronounced *ks*:

box → *boxer*	*fix* → *fixing*
mix → *mixes*	*relax* → *relaxed*

2. Regardless of where the stress falls in the word, a final *l* preceded by a single vowel sound written as a single letter is generally doubled:

appal → *appalling*	*counsel* → *counsellor*
propel → *propeller*	*rebel* → *rebelled*
jewel → *jewellery*	*cancel* → *cancellation*

The verb *parallel* is an exception to this rule. The final *l* does not double:

parallel → *paralleled*

And a final *l* does not usually double before *-ize*, *-ise*, *-ism*, *-ist* and *-ity*:

equal → equalize   special → specialist

final → finality   fatal → fatalism

There are however exceptions:

crystal → crystallize   tranquil → tranquillity

medal → medallist   panel → panellist

If the vowel sound before the *l* is written with a double letter, the *l* is not doubled (so it follows the general doubling rule):

sail → sailor   fool → fooling

But the *l* is doubled in *wool*, which goes against the doubling rule:

wool → woolly → woollen

3. Most verbs ending in *-p* follow the doubling rule, but three common ones do not, doubling the final *p* where, according to the stress pattern, you would not expect it:

worship → worshipped

handicap → handicapped

kidnap → kidnapping

4. Words ending in *-gram* double the final *m*:

program → programming   diagram → diagrammatic

5. A few words allow both single and double consonants. A good dictionary will show how these are spelt:

bias   bus   focus   gas   plus   yes

-e

When a word ends in *-e*, the general rule is to drop the *e* when adding a suffix beginning with a vowel:

smile → *smiling*	*white* → *whiter*
guide → *guidance*	*taste* → *tasting*

When adding a suffix beginning with a consonant, you do not need to drop the *e*:

move → *movement*	*use* → *useless*
concise → *conciseness*	*loose* → *loosely*

There are several exceptions to the rules for words ending in *-e*:

-ce, -ge
Keep the *e* after a soft *c* and *g* (pronounced with an *s* and *j* sound) when adding a suffix beginning with *a*, *o* or *u*:

advantage → *advantageous*

notice → *noticeable* (but *noticing*)

-ie
If a verbs ends in *-ie*, change this to *y* before adding *-ing*:

die → *dying*	*tie* → *tying*
lie → *lying*	*belie* → *belying*

-oe, -ee, -ye
If a verb ends in *-oe*, *-ee*, or *-ye*, keep the final *e* when adding any suffix, unless the suffix begins with an *e*:

agree → *agreeable* (but *agreed*)

dye → *dyeing* (but *dyed*)

hoe → *hoeing* (but *hoed*)

singe, swinge, route, tinge, etc
With some verbs, it is necessary to keep the final *e* when adding *-ing* to distinguish them from similar verbs that do not end in *-e*:

singe → *singeing*	(to distinguish it from *singing*)
swinge → *swingeing*	(to distinguish it from *swinging*)

SPELLING RULES

-le

If an adjective ends in -le and is preceded by a consonant, replace the final e with y to form the adverb:

simple → simply	single → singly
double → doubly	idle → idly

-dge

With words ending in -dge, it is correct to keep or drop the final e when adding a suffix:

judge → judgement or judgment

abridge → abridgement or abridgment

-y

When adding y to a word, keep the final e in words ending in -ue (glue → gluey) and these other words:

cage → cagey	dice → dicey
mate → matey	price → pricey

⚠ **Warning:** There are several other exceptions that you will simply need to remember:

due → duly	eerie → eerily
true → truly	whole → wholly
nine → ninth	acre → acreage
age → ageism	gay → gaily

-ed, -d

To form the past tense and past participle of most verbs, simply add -ed to the base form:

walk → walked	sail → sailed
toss → tossed	taxi → taxied
veto → vetoed	listen → listened

If the base form of the verb ends in -e, drop the e before adding -ed:

bake → *baked*   *change* → *changed*

agree → *agreed*   *glance* → *glanced*

If the base form of the verb ends in -y, change the y to i only if it is preceded by a consonant:

cry → *cried*   but   *stay* → *stayed*

⚠ **Warning:** Take care with the spelling of *laid*, *paid* and *said*, which are exceptions.

Words that end in -c usually add a k before -ed. See **-c**. For the rules about doubling final consonants when adding -ed or -d, see **Doubling final consonants**.

Adjectives

Adjectives ending in -ed and -d follow the same rules as the verbs:

red hair → *red-haired*   *beard* → *bearded*

leisure → *leisured*   *long leg* → *long-legged*

---

i

A **compound word** is made up of two or more whole words joined together, such as *bathroom*, *grasshopper*, *database* and *breakthrough*. It may help to remember the spelling of these words if you break them down into their separate parts, especially when there is a silent letter in the compound word, as in *cupboard*.

-ei-
See **i before e except after c**

-ence
See **-ance**

SPELLING RULES

-er, -est

In general, you add -er and -est to adjectives to form their comparatives and superlatives:

hard → *harder* → *hardest*

fast → *faster* → *fastest*

strong → *stronger* → *strongest*

When the adjective ends in -e, drop the final e before adding -er and -est:

white → *whiter* → *whitest*

simple → *simpler* → *simplest*

free → *freer* → *freest*

If the adjective ends in a single consonant, double the consonant when adding -er and -est if:
- the vowel preceding the consonant is written with a single letter
- the vowel and the consonant are part of a stressed syllable

red → *redder* → *reddest*

big → *bigger* → *biggest*

fat → *fatter* → *fattest*

If the adjective has two or more syllables and ends in -y, change the y to i before adding -er and -est:

angry → *angrier* → *angriest*

funny → *funnier* → *funniest*

happy → *happier* → *happiest*

> *Spelling Tip*
>
> Watch out for one-syllable adjectives ending in -y:
>
> *dry* → *drier* → *driest*
>
> *sly* → *slyer* or *slier* → *slyest* or *sliest*
>
> *shy* → *shyer* or *shier* → *shyest* or *shiest*
>
> And remember that some adjectives, like *good* have irregular comparative and superlative forms:
>
> *good* → *better* → *best*
>
> *bad* → *worse* → *worst*

-er, -or, -ar

The suffixes *-er*, *-or* and *-ar* can be added to words in English to form nouns meaning 'someone or something that...', for example *builder*, *sailor* and *beggar*. There is virtually no limit to the number of nouns that you can form in this way, and it can be difficult to know which ending to use. There are also many adjectives that end in *-ar* and some that end in *-or*. Unfortunately, there are no rules for these endings, but there are a few hints and tips that may help you choose the correct spelling.

As a possible clue to *-or* words, many of them are related to words that end in *-tion* or *-sion*:

acceleration → *accelerator*	*action* → *actor*
administration → *administrator*	*narration* → *narrator*
distribution → *distributor*	*collection* → *collector*
profession → *professor*	*oppression* → *oppressor*

If the word is an adjective, it will usually have the *-ar* ending:

angular	*molecular*	*perpendicular*	*singular*
circular	*muscular*	*popular*	*spectacular*
insular	*particular*	*regular*	*similar*

SPELLING RULES

As a clue for the *-ar* spellings, many of them are related to words that end in *-arity*:

circularity → *circular*   *popularity* → *popular*

Only a very small group of adjectives end in *-or*:

major	*minor*	*inferior*	*superior*
interior	*exterior*	*ulterior*	*tenor*

And many of these are related to words ending in *-ority*:

majority	*minority*	*inferiority*	*superiority*

If the word ends in an *-e*, drop the *e* when adding *-er*, *-or* or *-ar*:

bake → *baker*   *burgle* → *burglar*
contribute → *contributor*   *lie* → *liar*

If the word ends in a consonant followed by a *y*, change the *y* to *i*:

carry → *carrier*   but   *survey* → *surveyor*

> *Spelling Tip*
>
> Note that both *flier* and *flyer*, and *drier* and *dryer* are correct.

For the rules about doubling the final consonant when adding *-er*, *-or* or *-ar*, see **Doubling final consonants**. See also **-or** for how to spell words like *humour*, *colour* and *neighbour*.

-ery
See **-ary**

for-, fore-
The best way to decide how to spell a word beginning with the sound *for* is to think about what the word means. The prefix *fore-* means 'before', 'in front' or 'beforehand', so if the word you want to spell has anything to do with these ideas, the spelling will be *fore-*:

forehead	*foreboding*	*forecast*	*forefinger*
foreman	*foresee*	*foreshadow*	*forerunner*
forearm	*foretell*	*forefront*	*foreground*

The prefix *for-* means 'away', 'not', 'against' or 'utterly' but its meaning is not always obvious:

forbear	*forbid*	*forfeit*	*forget*
forgo	*forlorn*	*forsake*	*forswear*

-ful, al-, -til

When the word *full* becomes the suffix *-ful* it drops the final *l*:

hope → *hopeful*	*faith* → *faithful*
colour → *colourful*	*doubt* → *doubtful*

The same rule applies to the words *all* and *till*, which drop the final *l* when they are used as a prefix or suffix:

all → *already* → *altogether*

till → *until*

If the word that you are adding *-ful* to ends in *-y*, change the *y* to *i*:

beauty → *beautiful*	*pity* → *pitiful*
fancy → *fanciful*	*duty* → *dutiful*

> *Spelling Tip*
>
> Make sure you use the right spelling of *ful* to give the meaning you want:
>
> | *a handful of cherries* | = | as many cherries as fit in a hand |
> |---|---|---|
> | *a hand full of cherries* | = | a hand that contains cherries |

See also **-l**.

SPELLING RULES

i before e except after c

You will have probably heard the rule '*i* before *e* except after *c*'. The rule applies to words that have an *ee* sound, as in *deep*. After any letter except *c*, the *i* comes before the *e*:

bel*ie*ve	ch*ie*f	s*ie*ge	n*ie*ce
c*ei*ling	rec*ei*pt	perc*ei*ve	rec*ei*ve

There are some exceptions to this rule:

caffeine	counterfeit	protein	seize
skein	weir	weird	species

If the word is pronounced with an *ay* sound, as in *hay*, the spelling is usually *-ei-*:

eight	neighbour	weigh	vein

Words pronounced with a long *i* sound, as in *eye*, are usually spelt *-ei-*:

either	height	neither	sleight

There are some words where the *i* and the *e* produce a sound that is not *ee*, *ay* or *i*. If these letters come in the first syllable of a word, they are usually spelt *-ei-*:

their	heir

If the letters come towards the end of a word, they are almost always spelt *-ie-*:

ancient	efficient	patient	society

-ible
See **-able**

-ie-
See *i* **before** *e* **except after** *c*

-ing

To form the present participle of most verbs, simply add *-ing* to the base form:

walk → *walking*   *sing* → *singing*

stay → *staying*   *go* → *going*

If the base form of the verb ends in *-e*, drop the *e* before adding *-ing*:

bake → *baking*   *change* → *changing*

queue → *queuing*   *leave* → *leaving*

Exceptions are verbs ending in *-ee*, *-oe* and *-ye*:

agree → *agreeing*

hoe → *hoeing*

dye → *dyeing*

A few words keep the final *e* when adding *-ing*, to be distinguished from other similar words with no final *e*, for example *singe/singeing* as distinct from *sing/singing*.

One or two verbs can be spelt with or without the *e*:

age → *ageing* or *aging*   *cue* → *cueing* or *cuing*

If a verb ends in *-ie*, change this to *y* before adding *-ing*:

die → *dying*   *tie* → *tying*

Verbs that end in *-c* usually add a *k* before adding *-ing*. See **-c**. For the rules about doubling final consonants before adding *-ing*, see **Doubling final consonants**.

i

Silent vowels are sometimes used to control the sound of neighbouring consonants. The letters *g* and *c* usually have a hard sound before *a*, *o* and *u* (eg *gale*, *go* and *cup*) and a soft sound before *e*, *i* and *y* (eg *cell*, *ginger* and *mercy*). Some words have a silent *u* that keeps the sound hard before *e*, *i* or *y* (eg *guess*, *circuit* and *guy*). Some words have a silent *e* that keeps the sound soft before *a*, *o* or *u* (eg *noticeable*, *surgeon* and *pharmaceutical*).

-ise, -ize

Many verbs in British English can be spelt with *-ize* or *-ise*:

> *characterize* or *characterise*
>
> *realize* or *realise*
>
> *apologize* or *apologise*

There are some however that must always be spelt *-ise* and the difficulty is knowing which group a particular verb belongs to. So it is worth learning some of the common words that can only be spelt with *-ise* at the end:

advertise	*advise*	*arise*	*comprise*
compromise	*despise*	*devise*	*exercise*
improvise	*revise*	*rise*	*supervise*
surprise	*televise*		

There are also a few that are always spelt with *-ize* at the end:

capsize	*prize*	*size*

And remember that a few words are spelt *-yse*:

analyse	*breathalyse*	*catalyse*
electrolyse	*paralyse*	*psychoanalyse*

-l, -ll

Many people find it difficult to know whether to spell a word ending in *-l* with one or two *l*'s. Fortunately, there are a few guidelines that will help you choose the correct spelling.

If the word has only one syllable and the vowel is a single letter, the word will probably end in *-ll*:

all	*bill*	*call*	*chill*
dull	*fell*	*full*	*ill*
mill	*thrall*	*toll*	*will*

⚠ **Warning:** Exceptions to this rule are *gel*, *nil*, *pal* and *gal*.

If a word ends in *-ll*, you should of course keep this spelling when using it to form compound words:

call → *recall*		*fill* → *refill*
fall → *pitfall*		*mill* → *sawmill*

⚠ **Warning:** Exceptions to this rule are *annul*, *enrol*, *enthral* and *fulfil* (from *null*, *roll*, *thrall* and *full*).

If a word has more than one syllable, it will end with a single *l*:

appeal	*appal*	*distil*	*equal*
initial	*instil*	*model*	*prevail*
sandal	*symbol*	*final*	*evil*

For rules about doubling the final *l* when adding a suffix beginning with a vowel, see **Doubling final consonants**.

If a word ends in *-ll* and you want to add a suffix beginning with a consonant, drop one of the *l*'s:

dull	+ *-ly*	= *dully*
full	+ *-some*	= *fulsome*
install	+ *-ment*	= *instalment*

The exception is the suffix *-ness*:

dull	+ *-ness*	= *dullness*
ill	+ *-ness*	= *illness*

SPELLING RULES

⚠️ **Warning:** Take care when spelling these words:

    all → *almighty/almost/already/altogether*

    bell → *belfry*

    chill → *chilblain*

    well → *welfare*

See also **-ful**.

-ly

In English, you can often add the ending *-ly* to the end of an adjective to make an adverb:

    foolish → *foolishly*   *strange* → *strangely*

    surprising → *surprisingly*   *patient* → *patiently*

If an adjective ends in a consonant followed by *-le*, drop the final *e* and just add *y*:

    simple → *simply*   *double* → *doubly*

    subtle → *subtly*   *fiddle* → *fiddly*

For *true*, *due*, *whole* and *eerie*, drop the final *e* before adding *-ly*:

    true → *truly*   *due* → *duly*

    whole → *wholly*   *eerie* → *eerily*

If an adjective ends in a consonant followed by *y*, change the *y* to *i* when adding *-ly*:

    happy → *happily*   *weary* → *wearily*

⚠️ **Warning:** The following words can be spelt with a *y* or an *i*:

    dry → *dryly* or *drily*

    shy → *shyly* or *shily*

    sly → *slyly* or *slily*

If the adjective ends in *-ic*, add *-ally*:

basic → *basically*   *economic* → *economically*

There is one common exception to this: *public* → *publicly*.

Nouns

For forming plural nouns, see **Plurals**.

-oes

See **-os**

-or

See **-er**

---

i

The roots of many words come from Greek or Latin
words. For example, the root *spect*, found in *spectacle*,
spectator, *inspection* and *retrospect*, comes from a Latin
verb, meaning 'look at'. You may recognize some roots as
French words, for example *mort* meaning 'death', found
in *mortuary* and *immortal*, or *fin*, meaning 'end', found in
finish, *final*, *definite* and *infinity*.

-or, -our

Most 'doer' words – like *doctor*, *actor*, etc – end in *-or*, except *saviour*.
For more information about these 'doer' words, see **-er**.

There are however many more words that end in an *or* sound, but
the ending is spelt *-our*, such as *glamour* and *odour*. When you
add certain endings to these words, you drop the *u* in *-our*. These
endings include *-ant*, *-ary*, *-ation*, *-ial*, *-iferou*, *-ific*, *-ize*, or *-ise* and
-ous:

glamour → *glamorize*   *humour* → *humorous*

SPELLING RULES

honour → *honorary*	*colour* → *coloration*
odour → *odoriferous*	*armour* → *armorial*

Before other suffixes, leave the *u* in:

honour → *honourable*	*labour* → *labourer*
colour → *colourful*	*favour* → *favourite*
armour → *armoury*	*humour* → *humourless*

-ory
See **-ary**

-os, -oes
There are many words in British English that end in *-o* and it can be a problem knowing whether to add *s* or *-es* when forming plural nouns, like *studios*, or when forming the third person singular of verbs, for example *videos*. When considering verbs, if there is a related noun, simply add the ending that you would to the plural noun:

a veto → *several vetoes* → *she vetoes*

a radio → *several radios* → *she radios*

If the related noun allows both *-os* and *-oes*, add *-es*. If the verb does not have a related noun, just add *s*.

For more information about adding *s* and *-es* to nouns, see the section on **Plurals**.

-our
See **-or**

-ous, -us
You should be in no doubt about these two endings once you realize that the ending *-ous* is mainly used in adjectives and the ending *-us* is mainly used in nouns:

| famous | anonymous | enormous | poisonous |
| cactus | circus | octopus | thesaurus |

> *Spelling Tip*
>
> Some words which originally came into English from Latin, such as *emeritus*, are exceptions to this rule, because many Latin adjectives end in -*us*.

Plurals

Often plurals can be formed simply by adding *s*:

| *horse* → *horses* | *banana* → *bananas* |

If a nouns ends in -*ch*, -*sh*, -*s*, -*x*, or -*z*, add -*es*:

church → *churches*	*flash* → *flashes*
loss → *losses*	*box* → *boxes*
waltz → *waltzes*	

But if the final -*ch* is pronounced with a *k* sound, only add *s*:

| *stomach* → *stomachs* | *monarch* → *monarchs* |

You form the plural of some nouns ending in -*f* and -*fe* by changing the *f* or -*fe* to -*ve* before adding *s*:

| *scarf* → *scarves* | *hoof* → *hooves* |
| *knife* → *knives* | *shelf* → *shelves* |

But this is not always the case:

| *roof* → *roofs* | *belief* → *beliefs* |
| *chief* → *chiefs* | *proof* → *proofs* |

If a noun ends in a consonant followed by *y*, change the *y* to -*ie* then add *s*:

berry → *berries*	*hanky* → *hankies*
fly → *flies*	*cherry* → *cherries*

If the noun has a vowel before the *y*, simply add *s*:

boy → *boys*	*day* → *days*

Plurals of nouns ending in -*o* are often formed by just adding *s*:

piano → *pianos*	*radio* → *radios*
zoo → *zoos*	*solo* → *solos*

But some add -*es* instead:

potato → *potatoes*	*tomato* → *tomatoes*
hero → *heroes*	*echo* → *echoes*

And some can add either *s* or -*es*:

banjo → *banjos* or *banjoes*

domino → *dominos* or *dominoes*

manifesto → *manifestos* or *manifestoes*

(See also **-os**.)

⚠ **Warning:** There are many nouns that do not follow any of these rules and form their plurals irregularly:

foot → *feet*	*goose* → *geese*
tooth → *teeth*	*man* → *men*
mouse → *mice*	*child* → *children*
ox → *oxen*	*fish* → *fish*

Words which have come into English from other languages also often have plurals that do not follow these rules. This happens when the plural form is taken from the original language, which forms plurals in a different way from English:

cactus → *cacti*	*stimulus* → *stimuli*
helix → *helices*	*matrix* → *matrices*
formula → *formulae*	*vertebra* → *vertebrae*
criterion → *criteria*	*phenomenon* → *phenomena*
crisis → *crises*	*analysis* → *analyses*

Sometimes words that have come from other languages have two plural forms: one based on the original language, and one based on regular English spelling rules:

appendix → *appendixes* or *appendices*

stadium → *stadiums* or *stadia*

antenna → *antennas* or *antennae*

Words ending in *-eau* that have come from French have two plural forms: one (based on French spelling rules) ending in *-x*, and one (based on English spelling rules) ending in *-s*:

gateau → *gateaus* or *gateaux*

plateau → *plateaus* or *plateaux*

-se
See -ce

i

Knowledge of foreign root words, prefixes and suffixes can help you build up words and take them apart. For example, *auto* means 'self', *bio* means 'life' and *graph* means 'write'. So an autobiography is something someone writes about his or her own life. If you know that *hydro* means 'water' and *phobia* means 'fear', you should have no difficulty understanding or spelling the word *hydrophobia*.

SPELLING RULES

-sede
See -**cede**

-sion
See -**tion**

-sy
See -**acy**

-tion, -sion, -cion
To many people, there seems to be no logic to how the endings of words like *intention*, *extension*, *coercion* and *diversion* are spelt, and choosing the correct spelling can often end up as a guessing game. However, there are some very clear guidelines that will enable you to spell these words correctly with confidence.

Adding -cion
There are only two common words that end in *-cion*:

    coercion   *suspicion*

⚠ **Warning:** There are a large number of words that end in *-cian*, most of them describing a person's job:

magician	*mathematician*	*musician*
optician	*politician*	*technician*

Adding -tion or -sion
The best way to decide on the correct spelling is to first see whether or not the *-tion* or *-sion* ending follows a vowel or a consonant.

If the ending follows a **vowel** and is pronounced like the *z* in *seizure*, the spelling will be *-sion*:

adhesion	*decision*	*confusion*
division	*vision*	*seclusion*

If the ending follows a vowel and is pronounced like the *sh* sound in **shin**, the spelling will be *-tion*:

addition	education	nation
position	solution	translation

Exceptions are words that end in *-ssion*. These are easy to identify because they are based on words ending in *-ss*, *-mit* or *-cede*:

discuss → discussion

permit → permission

concede → concession

If an ending follows any **consonant** except *l*, *n* and *r*, the spelling will be *-tion*:

action	suggestion	option

After *l* the spelling will be *-sion*:

emulsion	expulsion	propulsion

After *n* and *r* the situation is a little less clear. In general, words related to or based on words ending in *-t* or *-tain* will be spelt *-tion*, and words related to or based on words ending in *-d* or *-se* will be spelt *-sion*:

assert → assertion	abstain → abstention
expand → expansion	immerse → immersion

⚠ **Warning:** Take care with these exceptions: *attention*, *contention* and *intention* (where the *-sion* ending would be expected); *conversion*, *diversion*, *extraversion* and *introversion* (where the *-tion* ending would be expected).

-us
See **-ous**

SPELLING RULES

Verbs

For the spelling of verb endings, see:

-ed
Doubling final consonants
-e
-c
-os
-y

-x
See **Plurals**

> **i**
>
> Knowledge of foreign words can help with spelling. The
> root *scien-*, which means 'knowing', is a difficult letter
> pattern that is found in words such as *science*, *scientific*,
> *conscience*, *conscientious* and *prescient*.

-y

Many English words end in *-y* and this can create spelling difficulties
when adding suffixes.

Nouns

To make a plural of a noun ending in *-y*, you generally change the
y to *-ies*:

cry → *cries*   *lady* → *ladies*

However, there are some exceptions:

For proper names, keep the final y and simply add *s*:

the two Germanys   *the four Marys*

Do the same for some compound nouns:

stand-bys   *lay-bys*

If the final *y* is preceded by a vowel, simply add *s*:

day → *days*	*buoy* → *buoys*
monkey → *monkeys*	*guy* → *guys*

Note that a *u* following a *q* is pronounced *w* and therefore counts as a consonant:

soliloquy → *soliloquies*

Verbs
Verbs follow the same pattern in that when the final *y* is preceded by a consonant, the *y* is changed to *i* and the suffix added:

cry → *cried*	*fly* → *flies*
vary → *variable*	*carry* → *carrier*

Note however that adding *-ing* will not change the spelling:

crying	*flying*	*varying*	*carrying*

And if the final *y* is preceded by a vowel, the spelling will not change when adding a suffix:

convey → *conveys*	*employ* → *employer*
obey → *obeying*	*enjoy* → *enjoyable*

⚠ **Warning:** Exceptions to this are *said*, *laid* and *paid*.

See also the spelling tip at **-er**.

Adjectives
You can make many common adjectives by simply adding *y* to a noun:

meat → *meaty*	*shadow* → *shadowy*

These adjectives follow the general rules for doubling consonants, dropping the final *e* and adding *k* to a final *c*:

grit → *gritty*

    ice → *icy*

    panic → *panicky*

For more information about these rules, see **Doubling final consonants**, **-e** and **-c**. For the spelling of comparative and superlative adjectives, like *sillier* and *silliest* (from silly), see **-er**, **-est**. For rules about adding *-ly* to words ending in *-y*, see **-ly**.

Adding other suffixes to words ending in -y
If the *y* is preceded by a consonant, change the *y* to *i* and add the suffix:

happy → *happiness*	*merry* → *merriment*
forty → *fortieth*	*pretty* → *prettiest*

When adding *-ness* to a word ending in *-ey*, change the *-ey* to *i* when the *-ey* is preceded by a consonant, and not when it is preceded by a vowel:

    cagey → *caginess*   *gluey* → *glueyness*

3 Difficult words

The following is an alphabetical list of words that many people find difficult to spell. For each word there is a note about what part of the word may trip you up, and often there is a reference to a relevant rule in the chapter on **Spelling rules** on pages 17–52. For some of the more difficult words, a special tip has been given to help you remember the spelling. You may find it more useful to make up some of your own tips for these and for other words you need to remember.

abandoned, abandoning
You do not need to double the *n* when adding *-ed* and *-ing* to *abandon*. This spelling follows the normal rules about doubling consonants.
▶ *Spelling rule*: **Doubling final consonants**.

abattoir
This has one *b* and double *t*, as in *b*eef and mu*tt*on.

abbreviate, abbreviation
This word is spelt with double *b*. Do not abbreviate it by omitting one of the *b*'s!

> *Spelling Tip*
>
> An a**bb**reviation is the **b**eginning **b**it of a word.

abhorrent
Note the double *r* and the *e*.

abscess
Be careful of the *-sc-* in the middle of this word.

absence
This word has an *s* in the middle and a *c* at the end.

abysmal, abysmally
Note the spelling *-bys-* of the second syllable and the double *l* in *abysmally*.
▶ *Spelling rule*: **-ly**.

academy
Note the *e* of the third syllable. It may help to remember that *academy* is related to *academic*.

accelerate, accelerator
This word is spelt with two *c*'s and one *l*. The ending of *accelerator* is *-or*.
▶ *Spelling rule*: **-er, -or, -ar**.

accessible
This word ends in *-ible*.
▶ *Spelling rule*: **-able, -ible**.

accessory
The ending of this word is spelt *-ory*, except in the specialist legal meaning, as in, for example, *an accessary after the fact*.
▶ *Spelling rule*: **-ary, -ery, -ory**.

accidentally
The ending is *-ally* because it is formed from *accidental* plus *-ly*.

accommodate, accommodation
Note the two *c*'s and two *m*'s.

> *Spelling Tip*
>
> The best a**cc**o**mm**odation has **c**omfortable **c**hairs and **m**odern **m**achines.

accumulate, accumulation, accumulator
All these words have two *c*'s but only one *m* and one *l*.

accuracy, accurate
These words have two *c*'s and one *r*, not the other way round.

achieve, achievement
Note that the *i* comes before *e* and that the *e* is kept before adding -*ment*.
▶ *Spelling rule*: ***i* before *e* except after *c*.**

acknowledge
It may help to remember that the core part of this word is *know*, with a *c* before it.

acquaint, acquaintance
Do not forget the *c* before the *q*.

acquiesce
Note the *c* before *q* and the -*sc*- towards the end.

> *Spelling Tip*
>
> To **acquiesce** means to **a**gree **c**almly, **quie**tly, and without making a **sc**ene.

acquire
Note the *c* before the *q*.

acquit, acquittal
Note the *c* before the *q* and the double *t* in *acquittal*.
▶ *Spelling rule*: **Doubling final consonants**.

DIFFICULT WORDS

acquisitive
Like *acquire*, this word has a *c* before the *q*. Note also the spelling -*sit*-. It may help to note the spelling of the related word, *acqui**sit**ion*.

across
There is only one *c* in this word.

> *Spelling Tip*
>
> To go a**cross** something is to **cross** it.

address
Note the two *d*'s in this word.

adequacy, adequate
Points to note in these words are the single *d*, the following *e* and the endings -*acy* and -*ate*.

adolescence, adolescent
Note the -*sc*- in these words, and the -*en*- towards the end.

advertise, advertisement, advertising
In British English, these words are always spelt -*ise*, never -*ize*.
▶ *Spelling rule*: **-ise, -ize**.

aerial
This begins with *ae*- and ends in -*al*.

> *Spelling Tip*
>
> With this **a**erial, **e**veryone **r**eceives **i**mportant **a**nnouncements **l**ive.

aerosol
Note the *ae*-.

affiliate, affiliation

These words are spelt with a double *f* and a single *l*.

aggravate, aggravating

Note the double *g* in these words.

aggression, aggressive

These words have two *g*'s and two *s*'s.

aghast

Take care not to omit the silent *h*. It may help to know that this word is related to **ghastly** and **ghost**.

align, alignment

The meaning of these words is related to *line*, but they are derived from French and so follow the French spelling *ligne*.

allege, allegation

Note the double *l* in these words. Remembering the spelling of either word will help you with the spelling of the other.

almond

Note the *l* before the *m*.

> *Spelling Tip*
>
> An **al**mond has an ov**al** shape.

amateur

This word has one *m* and -*eur* at the end.

anaesthetic

Note the -*ae*- in the middle.
▶ *Spelling rule*: -**ae**-, -**e**-.

analyse, analysis, analyst
Note the *y* in these words. In British English *analyse* must be spelt with an *s*, never a *z*.
▶ *Spelling rule*: **-ise, -ize**.

annihilate, annihilation
These words have two *n*'s, a silent *h* in the middle and only one *l*.

anonymous
Note the *y* in the middle of this word.

answer
This word has a silent *w* after the *s*. It may help to know that *an**sw**er* is related to the word ***sw**ear*.

Antarctic
As with the word *Arctic*, there is a *c* between the *r* and the *t*.

antibiotic, anticlimax
The prefix *anti-* has the meaning 'against, opposite', so this prefix, rather than *ante-*, is correct.
▶ *Spelling rule*: **ante-, anti-**.

apartheid
Note the *h* and the *-ei-*.

apologise, apology
Note the single *p* and the *-log-*. You can also spell *apologize* with a *z*.
▶ *Spelling rule*: **-ise, -ize**.

appalling
Note the double *p* and double *l*.
▶ *Spelling rule*: **Doubling final consonants**.

apparent
This word has two *p*'s and the ending is *-ent*.

appearance
This word has two p's and the ending is -ance.
▶ *Spelling rule*: **-ance, -ence**.

appreciate, appreciation
Note the double p.

arbitrary
The third syllable of this word is sometimes slurred in speech, so take care to include the -ar- in the middle when writing it.

architect, architecture
The -ch- in these words means the word begins with arch (think of an architect designing an arch).

Arctic
As with *Antarctic*, the c between the r and the t is often omitted in speech so take care to include it when writing.

argument
Note that the e of argue is dropped before -ment in argument, which goes against the general rule.
▶ *Spelling rule*: **-e**.

ascertain
Note the -sc-.

> *Spelling Tip*
>
> You try to **ascertain** something because you want to be **as certain** as possible about it.

asphyxiate, asphyxiation
Note the -ph- and the y.

DIFFICULT WORDS

aspirin
In speech, the *i* of the second syllable is often omitted, so take care to include it when writing the word.

assassin, assassinate
This word has two double *s*'s and one *n*.

assistance, assistant
These words have two *s*'s at the beginning and *a* in the ending.
▶ *Spelling rule*: **-ance, -ence**.

asthma
This word has a silent *-th-* in the middle.

atheist
This word is spelt with *-ei-* (not *-ie-*) in the middle. The pronunciation should help you with the spelling (ay-the**e**-**i**st).

attach
There is no *t* at the end of this word; the ending is *-ach*.

attendant
The ending of this word is spelt *-ant*.

autumn
This has a silent *n* at the very end, and it may help to think of the related word *autumnal* in which the *n* is clearly pronounced.

awful
There is no *e* in *awful*, which goes against the general rule for adding *-ful-* to words.
▶ *Spelling rule*: **-ful, al-, -til**.

bachelor
There is no *t* in this word.

baggage
Note the two *g*'s in the middle of this word, as in *luggage*.

balloon
This word has two *l*'s. It may help to remember that it has the word *ball* in it.

baptize, baptise
Both spellings are correct.

basically
Take care not to omit the *-al-* from this word.
▶ *Spelling rule*: **-ly**.

beautiful
This word has three vowels in the middle: *e*, *a* and *u*.

> *Spelling Tip*
>
> B**eau**tiful people are **e**legant **a**nd **u**nblemished.

belief, believe
These words start with *be-* and have *-ie-* (not *-ei-*) after the *l*.

belligerent
Note the double *l* and the *g*.

beneficial
Note the *c* in this word.

bias
The plural of this word is *biases*, with a single *s* in the middle, but the verb parts can be spelt with a single or double *s*: *biased*, *biassed*.

berserk
Note the *-er-* at the beginning of this word.

DIFFICULT WORDS

> *Spelling Tip*
>
> A rob**ber** and **ser**ial **k**iller have gone **berserk**.

biscuit
There is a *u* after the *c* in this word. It may help to know that the -*cuit* part of this word means 'cooked' and comes from the same root as French *cuisine*, meaning 'cooking'.

bizarre
This has one *z* and two *r*'s.

blancmange
It may help to know that this word comes from French: *blanc*, meaning 'white' and *manger*, meaning 'to eat'.

blasphemous, blasphemy
Note the -*ph*- in the middle of these words.

boundary
Note that this word ends in -*ary*.

bouquet
Note the -*ou*-, -*qu*- and -*et*.

bourgeois
Note the -*ou*-, -*ge*- and -*ois*.

boycott
This word ends in double *t*.

breadth
Take care not to forget the *a* in this word. It may help to remember that the breadth of something is how *broad* it is.

breath, breathe
The spelling of these two words should be easy to remember

because *breath* is the noun (*I lost my breath*) and *breathe* is the verb (*I couldn't breathe*).

brief
The *i* comes before the *e*, which follows the normal spelling rule.
▶ *Spelling rule*: *i* **before** *e* **except after** *c*.

broccoli
This word is often misspelt. It has two *c*'s and one *l*.

> *Spelling Tip*
>
> They serve bro**cc**oli with **c**ottage **c**heese and **oli**ves.

brochure
This is spelt with -*ch*- in the middle, even though it is pronounced with a *sh* sound.

Buddha, Buddhism, Buddhist
Note the position of the double *d* and the *h*.

buoyancy, buoyant
Like *buoy*, these words have a *u* before the *o*. It may help to note that both these words have *you* written backwards in them,.

bureau
Note the -*eau*. The plural can be *bureaux* or *bureaus*.

bureaucracy, bureaucratic
Both these words have the word *bureau* in them, and this may help you remember their spelling.
▶ *Spelling rule*: -**acy, -asy**.

burglar
This is one of the few 'doer' words that ends in -*ar*.
▶ *Spelling rule*: -**er, -or, -ar**.

buses, bused, busing

These usually only have one *s* in the middle. Forms with double *s* are correct, but are now very rare.

business

This word has an unpronounced *i* in the middle. It may help to know that the word is spelt as if it were formed from *busy*, which historically it is, but the *y* has changed to an *i*.

caffeine

The *-ei-* spelling of this word does not follow the general rule.
▶ *Spelling rule*: *i* **before** *e* **except after** *c*.

calendar

The second syllable is an *e* and the last syllable is an *a*, not the other way round.

> *Spelling Tip*
>
> A cal**e**nd**a**r shows the days of the y**ea**r.

camouflage

This word has *-ou-* in the middle and *-age* at the end.

campaign

Note the *-ai-* and the silent *g*.

carburettor

Note the double *t* in this word. The spelling *carburetter* is also correct, but the *-or* spelling is more common.

career

There is only one *r* in the middle of this word.

Caribbean

This has only one *r* and two *b*'s.

carriage
This word has two *r*'s followed by an *i*.

cassette
Note the two *s*'s and two *t*'s.

casual, casually, casualty
Note the -*ua*- in the middle of these words. If you pronounce the *u* when you say the word, you will spell it correctly.

catarrh
This word has a very unusual spelling. The -*rrh* ending comes from a Greek word meaning 'running, flowing' and is also found in the words *diarrhoea* and *haemorrhage*.

ceiling
The -*ei*- spelling of this word follows the normal spelling rule.
▶ *Spelling rule*: **i before e except after c**.

cemetery
Take care to remember the *e* in the last syllable as this is not usually pronounced in speech.

> *Spelling Tip*
>
> There's a **meter** in the ce**meter**y.

changeable
Note that the *e* is not dropped when adding the -*able* ending.
▶ *Spelling rule*: **-able, -ible**.

chasm
Note the initial *ch*-.

chauffeur
Note the -*au*-, double *f* and the -*eu*-.

DIFFICULT WORDS

chief, chiefly
The -ie- spelling of these words follows the normal spelling rule.
▸ *Spelling rule*: **i before e except after c**.

chimneys
This plural is formed by simply adding *s* to *chimney*.
▸ *Spelling rule*: **-y** for more information on forming plurals of words ending in -*y*.

chronically
Note the *ch-* at the beginning and the -*al*- before the -*ly* ending.
▸ *Spelling rule*: **-ly**.

chute
This word is spelt with *ch-*, not *sh-* as you might expect.

cocoa
Note the final *a*.

coconut
This word is not related to *cocoa* and there is no *a* in it.

collaborate, collaborator
This word has two *l*'s and one *b*. To *collaborate* means to work with someone, the meaning coming from *col-* (a form of the Latin word meaning 'with') and *labor* (work). The core word is the same as words like *laborious* and *laboratory*.
▸ *Spelling rule*: **-er, -or, -ar**.

collapsible
Note the double *l* and the ending -*ible*.
▸ *Spelling rule*: **-able, -ible**.

college
Note that there is no *d* in the ending -*ege*.

colossal

This word is tricky as it has a single *l* but double *s*.

> *Spelling Tip*
>
> Co**loss**al **loss**es cause bankruptcy.

commemorate

This has two *m*'s, then a single *m*. It may help to know that the core of this word is the same as that of *memory* and *memorial* to which *com*- has been added.

commitment

A common mistake is to double the *t* of *commit* when forming this word.

▶ *Spelling rule*: **Doubling final consonants**.

committed, committing

Note that you need to double the final *t* of *commit*.

▶ *Spelling rule*: **Doubling final consonants**.

committee

This word has two *m*'s, two *t*'s and two *e*'s.

> *Spelling Tip*
>
> A co**mm**i**tt**ee is a **t**hink **t**ank with **m**any **m**embers.

comparative

Note the *a* of the third syllable.

comparison

Note the difference in spelling between *comparison* and *comparative*.

compatible

This ends in -*ible*.

▶ *Spelling rule*: **-able, -ible**.

DIFFICULT WORDS

competitive, competitor
If you are in doubt about the *i* of the third syllable, think of the related word *competition*, in which the *i* is clearly pronounced. Note also that *competitor* is one of the 'doer' words that end in *-or*.

complexion
This is one of very few words that end in *-xion* rather than *-ction*.

concede
Note the spelling of the ending *-cede*.
▶ *Spelling rule*: **-cede, -ceed, -sede**.

conceit, conceited
The *-ei-* spelling of these words follows the normal spelling rule.
▶ *Spelling rule*: *i* **before** *e* **except after** *c*.

connection
This is the usual spelling if this word, although *connexion* is also correct.

connoisseur
This word is full of potential pitfalls! This tip should help you spell it correctly:

> *Spelling Tip*
>
> A co**nn**oisseur makes **no noi**se when **s**ilently **s**ipping **Eur**opean wine.

conscience
The core of this word is *science*, although the pronunciation is different.

conscientious
This word is related to *conscience*, but note that the *c* changes to *t* in *conscientious*.

68

conscious
Note the *-sci-* in the middle of this word, as in con**sci**ence and con**sci**entious.

consensus
Many people are unsure about how many *c*'s and *s*'s this word should have.

> *Spelling Tip*
>
> It makes **sens**e to agree with the rest of **us** – let's have a con**sensus**.

contemporary
The *o* in this word is often slurred in speech, so take care to include it when writing it.

controversial
Note the spelling is *contro-*, not *contra-*. It may help to think of the related word contr**o**versy.

convalescence, convalescent
Note the *-val-*, the *-sc-* and the *-en*.

convertible
Note that the ending is *-ible*, not *-able*.
▶ *Spelling rule*: **-able, -ible**.

coolly
This follows the normal spelling rule; simply add *-ly* to the adjective *cool* to make the adverb *coolly*.

coronary
Some people tend to write this word with three *o*'s, whereas the third syllable is spelt with an *a*.

DIFFICULT WORDS

correspondence, correspondent
Note the double *r* and the *-en-*.

counterfeit
Note that the ending is *-ei-* not *-ie-*, which goes against the normal spelling rule.
▶ *Spelling rule*: *i* before *e* except after *c*.

courageous
Note that the *e* is kept before the *-ous* ending, which enables the *g* to remain the soft *j* sound you hear in *courage*.

courteous
Note the *e* before the ending *-ous*. It may help to note that there is an *e* in the related word *court*e*sy*.

critically
This should not pose a problem if you remember that this is simply the adjective *critical* made into the adverb *critically* by following the normal spelling rule and adding *-ly*.

crochet, crocheted, crocheting
The word *crochet* is taken from French, hence the *-ch-* spelling for the *sh* sound and the unpronounced final *t*.

crucifixion
This is one of very few words that end in *-xion* rather than *-ction*.

cruelly
This is simply the adjective *cruel* made into the adverb *cruelly* by following the normal spelling rule and adding *-ly*.

cryptic
Note the *y* in the middle of this word. It may help to know that this word comes from the Greek *kryptos*, meaning 'hidden'.

currency
Note the double *r* and the *-en*.

curriculum
Only the *r* is doubled in this word. All the other consonants are single letters.

cylinder
Note the *cy-* and the ending *-er*.

daffodil
This is spelt with two *f*'s but only one *d* and one *l*.

deceit, deceitful, deceive
The *-ei-* spelling of these words follows the normal spelling rule.
▸ *Spelling rule*: **i before e except after c**.

defence, defensive
Note that the noun is spelt with a *c* and the adjective is spelt with an *s*. *Defense* is correct in both cases in American English.

defendant
Note the ending *-ant*.

definite, definitely
The *i* of the second syllable is often slurred in speech, so take care not to omit it when writing these words. It may help to remember that these words contain the word *finite*.

deliberate
Note the *de-* and the *-be-*.

demeanour
Note the *-our* ending.
▸ *Spelling rule*: **-or, -our**.

DIFFICULT WORDS

deodorant
There is no *u* in *deodorant*. The *o* of the related word *odour* drops before the *-ant* ending.
▶ *Spelling rule*: **-or, -our**.

descend, descendant
Note the *-sc-* in the middle of these words and the ending *-ant* in *descendant*.

describe, description
Note the *des-* spelling at the beginning.

desiccated
This is spelt with one *s* and two *c*'s, not the other way round as you might expect. It may help to remember *desi**cc**ated **co**conut*.

despair
This word begins with *des-*. If in doubt, think of ***des**peration*.

desperate
There is an *e* between the *p* and the *r* and the ending is *-ate*.

> *Spelling Tip*
>
> **Per**il is a des**perate** st**ate**.

despise
This word should always be spelt with *-ise* at the end, never *-ize*.
▶ *Spelling rule*: **-ise, -ize**.

detach, detached
There is no *t* before the *-ch-* in these words.

deterrent
Note the double *r*.
▶ *Spelling rule*: **Doubling final consonants**.

develop

There is no *e* at the end of *develop*.

developed, developing

You do not need to double the *p* before adding *-ed* and *-ing*.

▶ *Spelling rule*: **Doubling final consonants**.

development

As there is no *e* at the end of *develop*, there is no *e* between the *p* and the *m* in *development*.

diaphragm

Note the *-ph-* and the silent *g*.

diarrhoea

This word has a very unusual spelling. The *-rrh-* in the middle of the word comes from a Greek word meaning 'running, flowing' and is also found in the words *catarrh* and *haemorrhage*.

> *Spelling Tip*
>
> Dia**rrh**oea may be caused by **o**v**erea**ting and may make you **r**un **r**apidly **h**ome!

dilemma

This has one *l* and two *m*'s.

diphtheria

Note the *-ph-*.

disappear

This word has one *s* and two *p*'s and is formed from *dis-* plus *appear*.

disappoint

This has one *s* and two *p*'s and is formed from *dis-* plus *appoint*.

DIFFICULT WORDS

disastrous
Note that there is no *e* in *disastrous*. The *e* of *disaster* is dropped before adding the ending *-ous*.

discipline, disciplinary
Note the *-sc-* the middle, and the ending *-ary*.

discrepancy
Note the *-an-* spelling at the end of the word.

dispatch, despatch
Both these spellings are correct but the *dis-* spelling is more common.

dissatisfaction
This is simply *dis-* plus *satisfaction*, hence the double *s*.

dissect
There is a double *s* in this word, although because of the pronunciation you would only expect one.

dissent
Note the double *s* in this word.

dissimilar
This is simply *dis-* plus *similar*, hence the double *s*.

dissolve
Note the double *s* in this word, although because of the pronunciation you would only expect one.

drunkenness
This has a double *n* because it is formed from *drunken* plus the ending *-ness*.

dryer, drier
Both spellings are correct when the word is a noun. *Drier* is correct for the comparative adjective meaning 'more dry'.

dryly, drily

Both spellings are correct.

duly

The *e* of *due* is dropped when adding *-ly*, which goes against the rule for adding *-ly*.

▶ *Spelling rule*: **-e**.

earnest

Note the *ear-* spelling at the beginning of the word.

earring

This has a double *r* in the middle because it is a compound noun made up of the words *ear* and *ring*.

eccentric

Note the double *c* in this word. The pronunciation should help you spell it correctly, with *ec-* representing the *ek* sound and *-cen-* representing the *sen* sound.

ecstasy

Note the *-cs-* and the ending *-asy*.

> *Spelling Tip*
>
> **E**veryone **c**an **s**pell **t**his e**asy** word.

eczema

This is a very unusual spelling and many people find it difficult to remember the *-cz-* and the middle *e*. When writing this word, it may help to sound out the word as it is spelt: ek-zem-a.

eighth

This has only one *t*, although the pronunciation might lead you to expect two.

DIFFICULT WORDS

eligible, eligibility
This word is all *l*'s and *i*'s; note the *-lig-* and the *-ible*, *-ibility*.
▶ *Spelling rule*: **-able, -ible**.

embarrass, embarrassed, embarrassing, embarrassment
These words have an embarrassment of double *r*'s and double *s*'s!

encyclopaedia, encyclopedia
Both are correct, but the spelling without the middle *a* is now more common.

endeavour
Note the *-ea-* in the middle and the *-our* ending.
▶ *Spelling rule*: **-or, -our**.

enrol, enrolment
There is only one *l* in these words, but the *l* is doubled in *enrolled* and *enrolling*.
▶ *Spelling rule*: **Doubling final consonants**.

environment
This has the word *iron* in it; this will help you remember the spelling.

equalize, equalise
The final *l* of the base word *equal* does not double when adding *-ise* or *-ize*.
▶ *Spelling rule*: **Doubling final consonants**.

erroneous
This has double *r*, as in *error*. Note also the ending *-eous*, which is what you would expect from the way the word is pronounced.

etiquette
This has one *t* at the beginning and two at the end.

exaggerate, exaggeration
This word has two *g*'s in the middle.

> *Spelling Tip*
>
> A br**agger** will always ex**agger**ate.

exceed, exceeding, exceedingly
Note the *-ceed* spelling of this word.
▶ *Spelling rule*: **-cede, -ceed, -sede**.

excellent, excellence
This has *exc-* at the beginning, two *l*'s in the middle and the ending is *-ent*.

excerpt
Take care not to omit the *c* and the *p*.

> *Spelling Tip*
>
> They always show a **cer**tain **p**art as an ex**cerpt**.

excise
This is one of the words whose ending can never be written *-ize*.

excite, exciting, excited
Take care not to omit the *c* in these words – this is a common mistake.

exercise
The ending of this word can never be written *-ize*.

exhaust, exhaustion
Note the silent *h* after the *ex-*.

exhibit, exhibition
Note the silent *h* after the *ex-*.

DIFFICULT WORDS

exhilarate, exhilaration
Don't forget the silent *h* in these words. Note also the spelling *-lar-*. It may help to know that the base of these words is the same as the base of **hilar**ious and **hilar**ity, where the *a* is more clearly pronounced.

exhort, exhortation
Don't forget the silent *h* in these words.

expense
This word ends in *-se*, not *-ce*. It may help to remember how *expen**s**ive* is spelt.

extension
This word ends in *-sion*. If in doubt, think of *exten**s**ive*.

extraordinary
Don't forget the *a* of *extra-* in this word. The word is formed from *extra-* plus *ordinary*, but the *a* sound is not usually pronounced in speech.

extravagance, extravagant
Note the *a*'s in *-vagance* and *-vagant*.

extravert, extrovert
Both spellings are correct but the form with *o* is now more common.

facetious
Note that the ending of this word is spelt *-tious*.

fallible
Note that the ending of this word is spelt *-ible*, not *-able*.
▶ *Spelling rule*: **-able, -ible**.

fascinate, fascination
This word is spelt with *-sc-* in the middle.

Spelling Tip

Science fa**sci**nates me.

favour, favourite
Both are spelt with *-ou* in British English.

feasible
The ending of this word is spelt *-ible*, not *-able*.
▶ *Spelling rule*: **-able, -ible**.

February
Take care with the spelling of *-ruary*, which is usually not clearly pronounced in speech.

fiancé, fiancée
Your *fiancé* is the man you are going to marry, and your *fiancée* is the woman you are going to marry.

fiery
Although this word sounds like *fire* and is related to it in meaning, the spelling is *-ier-*, not *-ire-*.

fluorescent
Note the *u* and the *-sc-*.

Spelling Tip

You get **flu**, **ore** and **scent** from the word **fluorescent**.

fluoride
Note the *u* in this word.

focus
The plural of the noun is spelt with one *s*, *focuses*, but you can form the verb endings using a single or double *s*: *focused* or *focussed*, *focusing* or *focussing*.

▶ *Spelling rule*: **Doubling final consonants**.

foreboding
This is spelt *fore-*, not *for-*.
▶ *Spelling rule*: **for-, fore-**.

foreign, foreigner
The spelling is *-ei-*, with a silent *g* before the *n* at the end.

forfeit
Note the *-ei-* at the end, which goes against the normal spelling rule.
▶ *Spelling rule*: *i* **before** *e* **except after** *c*.

forgo
This is spelt exactly as the meaning of the prefix *for-*, 'do without', would suggest.
▶ *Spelling rule*: **for-, fore-**.

forty
There is no *u* in *forty*, but this word is commonly misspelt because of the related word *fo**u**r*.

friend
The *-ie-* spelling of this word follows the normal spelling rule.
▶ *Spelling rule*: *i* **before** *e* **except after** *c*.

fulfil, fulfilment
These words are spelt with a single *l* in British English.

fulfilled, fulfilling
The final *l* of *fulfil* is doubled before *-ed* and *-ing*.
▶ *Spelling rule*: **Doubling final consonants**.

gaiety, gaily
Note that the *y* of *gay* becomes *i* in these words.

gaol
This is a very unusual spelling so, if in doubt, use *jail* instead.

gas
You do not double the *s* when forming the plural noun *gases*. However, the *s* is doubled for the verb forms: *gasses*, *gassed*, *gassing*.
▶ *Spelling rule*: **Doubling final consonants**.

gateau
The plural can be *gateaux* or *gateaus*.

gauge
The *u* comes after, not before, the *a*.

> *Spelling Tip*
>
> To **gauge** is to **g**et **a u**seful **g**eneral **e**stimate.

genuine
This word has an *e* at the end. It may help to mentally pronounce the word 'jen-yoo-ine' rather than 'jen-yoo-in' when you are writing it.

ghastly
Remember the silent *h*.

ghetto
Remember the silent *h*. The plural is *ghettos*.
▶ *Spelling rule*: **-os, -oes**.

ghost
Remember the silent *h*.

Gipsy, Gypsy
Both spellings are correct, but the *y* spelling is more common.

DIFFICULT WORDS

glamorize, glamorous
The *u* is dropped from *glamour* before *-ize* and *-ous*. *Glamorise* can also be spelt with an *s*.
▶ *Spelling rule*: **-ise, -ize**.

gorgeous
Note the *e* in the middle of this word.

> *Spelling Tip*
>
> Let me **gorge** myself on this **gorge**ous food.

gossiping, gossipy
You do not double the *p* of *gossip* when adding a suffix.
▶ *Spelling rule*: **Doubling final consonants**.

government
There is an *n* in *government* (remember, the government *gove**rn**s*), although it is not pronounced in speech.

governor
Note that this ends in *-or*.

graffiti
This word has two *f*'s and one *t*.

grammar
A common mistake when writing this word is to spell it with *-er* at the end. It may help to think of the related word *gramm**a**tical*.

grandeur
Note the *-eur* spelling at the end.

gray, grey
In British English, the usual spelling is *grey*, and although *gray* is correct, it is less common and is the standard American English spelling.

grief, grieve, grievance

The -ie- spelling of these words follows the normal spelling rule.
▶ *Spelling rule: **i** before **e** except after **c**.*

grievous

There is no *i* before the -ous ending. Just think of how the word is pronounced (gree-vus) and you won't go wrong.

gruesome

Don't forget the *e* of *grue-*.

guarantee

There is only one *r*, and don't forget the *u* after the *g*.

gullible

This word ends in -ible, which is not what you might expect from the general rule.
▶ *Spelling rule: **-able, -ible**.*

Gypsy, Gipsy

Both spellings are correct, but the *y* spelling is more common.

haemorrhage

Take care with the -ae-, the single *m* and the -rrh. The -rrh in the middle of the word comes from a Greek word meaning 'running, flowing' and is also found in the words *catarrh* and *diarrhoea*.

handkerchief

Notice that this word begins with *hand-*, although the *d* is usually not pronounced in speech.

harangue

Note the single *r* and the final -ue.

harass

This has one *r* and double *s*. Note the difference in spelling between *harass* and *embarrass*.

DIFFICULT WORDS

hazard
This word has only one *z*.

height
Although this word is related to *high*, it has as an *e* in it before the *i*.
▶ *Spelling rule*: **i before e except after c**.

heir, heiress
Note the silent *h* and the *-ei-* in these words.
▶ *Spelling rule*: **i before e except after c**.

herbaceous
This word has an *e* after the *c* and this is what creates the *sh* sound.

hereditary
The *a* at the end of this word is not pronounced in speech, so take care not to omit it when writing it.

hiccup, hiccough
Both spellings are correct, but the first is more common. You do not need to double the *p* when adding *-ed* or *-ing* to *hiccup*.
▶ *Spelling rule*: **Doubling final consonants**.

hindrance
The *e* of *hinder* is dropped in this word, and it is spelt as you would pronounce it.

honorary
The *-ar-* is often not pronounced or is slurred in speech, so take care not to omit it when writing it.

honourable
You should not drop the *u* of *honour* before the ending *-able*.
▶ *Spelling rule*: **-or, -our**.

humorous

The ending is -ous, but you should drop the u from the word *humour* before adding the ending.

hygiene, hygienic

The -ie- spelling of this word follows the normal spelling rule. But note also the y.

▶ *Spelling rule:* **i before e except after c**.

> *Spelling Tip*
>
> **Y**ou can **g**et **ill** without **e**ffective h**ygie**ne.

hypocrisy

Note the y after the h at the beginning and the i. It may help to think of the related words *hypocrite* and *hypocritical*.

hypocrite

The ending is -ite; don't forget the e at the end!

hysterically

Note the y of the first syllable. Notice also that the word ends in -ally; this is formed simply by adding -ly to *hysterical*.

idiosyncrasy

Many people find this word difficult to spell correctly because of the -asy ending, but thinking of the related word *idiosyncratic* will help you remember the a.

▶ *Spelling rule:* **-acy, -asy**.

illegal

This has two l's at the beginning because it is formed from *legal* plus the prefix il-, meaning 'not'.

illiterate

This has two l's at the beginning because it is formed from *literate* plus the prefix il-, meaning 'not'.

DIFFICULT WORDS

imaginary
Note the *-ary* ending. It may help to think of the related word *imagination*.

immediate, immediately
These words are spelt with double *m*.

immense
Note the double *m*.

immigrant, immigration
This word is formed from *migrant* and the prefix *im-*, which is used instead of *in-* with words beginning with *b*, *m* or *p* to mean 'into' hence migration into a country.

immoral
This word is formed from the prefix *im-*, meaning 'not' and *moral*.

immortal
This word is formed from the prefix *im-*, meaning 'not' and *mortal*.

impostor
Be careful with the ending of this word; it is spelt *-or*, not *-er*.

improvise
This is always spelt *-ise*, never *-ize*.
▶ *Spelling rule*: **-ise, -ize**.

incredible
Notice that the ending is spelt *-ible*, not *-able*.
▶ *Spelling rule*: **-able, -ible**.

indefinitely
Thinking of the related word *finite* should help you spell this word correctly.

independent

The ending of this word is -ent, not -ant.
▶ *Spelling rule*: spelling tip at **-ance, -ence**.

> *Spelling Tip*
>
> Every flat has its own independ**ent ent**rance.

indestructible

Note the ending -ible.
▶ *Spelling rule*: **-able, -ible**.

indict, indictment

Both these words have a silent *c*.

inexhaustible

Note the silent *h* and the ending -ible.
▶ *Spelling rule*: **-able, -ible**.

infallible

The ending of this word is -ible.
▶ *Spelling rule*: **-able, -ible**.

inflammable

This word has a double *m* and ends in -able, not -ible. It may help to think of the related word *inflammation*.
▶ *Spelling rule*: **-able, -ible**.

innocent

Note the double *n*.

innumerable

This word means 'so great as to be not (*in-*) *numerable*', hence the double *n*.

inoculate, inoculations

There is only one *n* and one *c* in these words.

DIFFICULT WORDS

inseparable
Note the *-par-*. It may help to think of the meaning, *never a**part***.

install, instal
Both spellings are correct, but *install* is more common in British English.
▶ *Spelling rule*: **-l, -ll**.

instalment
There is only one *l* before the *-ment* ending.

> *Spelling Tip*
>
> An inst**alment** is **a** **l**ittle **m**onthly paym**ent**.

instil
This word ends in a single *l*.

interrogate, interrogation
Note the double *r* in this word.

interrupt, interruption
Note the double *r* in this word.

irascible
This word has a single *r*. It may help to think of the related words *ire* and *irate*.

irregular
This word is formed from the prefix *ir-*, meaning 'not', and *regular*, hence the double *r*.

irrelevant
This word is formed from the prefix *ir-*, meaning 'not', and *relevant*, hence the double *r*.

irresistible

This word is formed from the prefix *ir-*, meaning 'not', and *resistible*, hence the double *r*. Note also the ending *-ible*.
▶ *Spelling rule*: **-able, -ible**.

irresponsible

This word is formed from the prefix *ir-*, meaning 'not', and *responsible*, hence the double *r*. The ending is *-ible*.
▶ *Spelling rule*: **-able, -ible**.

irritable, irritate, irritation

This word has two *r*'s and the ending is *-able*.
▶ *Spelling rule*: **-able, -ible**.

itinerary

The *-ar-* part of this word is often slurred in speech, so take care not to omit it when writing.

jealous

Note the *-ea-* after the *j*.

jeopardise, jeopardy

Be careful not to omit the *o* in this word. *Jeopardize* may also be spelt with a *z*.
▶ *Spelling rule*: **-ise, -ize**.

jewellery

The final *l* of *jewel* is doubled before the ending *-ery* is added. It is spelt with one *l* in American English.
▶ *Spelling rule*: **Doubling final consonants**.

judgement, judgment

Both spellings are correct, but *judgement* is now more common.

kidnapped, kidnapping, kidnapper
Kidnap is an exception to the doubling rule because the *p* is doubled when adding a suffix.

▶ *Spelling rule*: **Doubling final consonants**.

knowledgeable
The *e* of *knowledge* is kept when adding *-able*.

> *Spelling Tip*
>
> Do you **know** that there's a **ledge** in **knowledge**able?

laboratory
Note the spelling of the ending *-atory*, which is often slurred in speech.

labyrinth
Note the *y*, which is often slurred in speech.

lacquer
Note the position of the *c*, the *-qu-* and the *e*.

language
Take care to put the *u* in the correct place; it goes before (not after) the *a*.

languor, languorous
Note the position of the unpronounced *u* in these words. It may help to remember that these words are related to *languid*, in which the *u* is pronounced, albeit as a *w* sound.

lasagne, lasagna
Either spelling is correct.

lascivious
Take care to remember the *-sc-* in the middle of this word.

launderette
The e of the core word *launder* is kept in this word, although it is often not pronounced in speech. It is interesting to note that the e is dropped in *laundry*.

leisure
The -ei- spelling of this word goes against the normal spelling rule.
▶ *Spelling rule: i before e except after c.*

liaise, liaison
This is a very unusual spelling, and it is easy to omit one of the i's.

> *Spelling Tip*
>
> You need two eyes (i's) to liaise properly.

library
The middle syllable of this word is sometimes not pronounced or is slurred in speech. It will help to think of the related word *librarian*, in which the -ra- is clearly pronounced.

lieutenant
Be careful with the spelling of the first syllable of this word, *lieu-*.

liquefy
This is one of the few words in the English language which end in -efy.

liqueur
There are two u's in this word, each either side of the e.

liquor
Note the difference in spelling between this word and *liqueur*.

literate, literature
Take care to remember the e between the t and the r in the middle of this word. There are no double t's.

DIFFICULT WORDS

luggage

Like *baggage*, this word has double *g* in the middle.

magnanimous

Notice the *i* of *-animous*. It may help to think of the related word *magnanimity*, in which the *i* is clearly pronounced, or to know that this part of the word comes from the Latin **anim**us, meaning 'mind'.

maintenance

Note the *e* in the middle of this word, and the ending *-ance*.

manageable

The *e* of the core word *manage* is kept before adding *-able*, in order to keep the soft *j* sound of the *g*.

manoeuvre

Note the three vowels, *-oeu-*, in the middle of this word, and the ending *-vre*.

> *Spelling Tip*
>
> I ma**noeuvr**ed my ca**noe u**p the **v**iolent **r**apids.

margarine

In spite of the soft *j* sound of the letter *g*, the vowel after *g* is *a*, not *e* as you might expect.

marriage

Remember that this has two *r*'s, followed by *i*.

martyr

Note that the ending is *-tyr*.

marvellous

The *l* of *marvel* is doubled before adding *-ous*.
▶ *Spelling rule*: **Doubling final consonants**.

marzipan
Note that this word is spelt with an *i*, not an *e*, in the middle.

massacre
Note the double *s* in the middle and the *-re* spelling at the end.

mayonnaise
This word is spelt with double *n*.

medallist
The *l* of *medal* is doubled before adding *-ist*.
▸ *Spelling rule*: **Doubling final consonants**.

medicine
Take care not to omit the first *i* in the word, which is often not pronounced in speech. It may help to remember the related word *medicinal*, in which the *i* is clearly pronounced.

medieval, mediaeval
Both spellings are correct, but the first spelling is now more common in British English, and is standard in American English.

Mediterranean
This word means 'in the middle of the land': *medi-* is connected with *medium*, and *terra* is connected with *terrain* and *terrestrial*.

meringue
The pronunciation of this word reflects its French origins, as does its spelling. Saying the word as it is spelt may help you to write it correctly (mer-ing-yew).

meteorology, meteorologist, meteorological
The core of these words is *meteor*, but the *e* is often slurred or not pronounced at all in speech, so take care not to omit it when writing.

DIFFICULT WORDS

milage, mileage
Both spellings are correct.

millennium
This word has two *l*'s and two *n*'s. It may help to know that this word is based on root words meaning 'a thousand' and 'years'. The same roots are found in the words *mil**l**imetre* and *a**nn**ual*.

millionaire
This word has two *l*'s but only one *n*.

miniature
Note the *a* after *mini-*.

> *Spelling Tip*
>
> She wore a **mini** skirt **at** the party.

minuscule
This word is often misspelt; take care to spell it with a *u* in the second syllable, not an *i*. If in doubt, think of the related word *min**u**te*, meaning 'tiny'.

miraculous
Note the single *l* in this word.

miscellaneous
This word has *sc-* at the beginning, two *l*'s in the middle, and the ending is *-eous*.

mischief, mischievous
This is spelt *-ie-* in the middle, not *-ei-*. It may help to remember that *mischief* has the word *chief* in it.
▶ *Spelling rule*: *i* **before** *e* **except after** *c*.

misshapen
This word is formed from *mis-*, meaning 'badly', and *shape*, hence the double *s*.

misspell, misspelt
These words are formed from *mis-*, meaning 'badly', and *spell*, *spelt*, hence the double *s*.

misspent
This word is formed from *mis-*, meaning 'badly', and *spent*, hence the double *s*.

moccasin
There are two *c*'s and one *s* in this word.

mortgage
Note the *t* in this word.

naïve, naive
It is equally correct to write this word with or without the diaeresis (the two small dots) over the *i*.

> *Spelling Tip*
>
> **Naï**ve people are **a**wfully **i**nexperienced.

necessary, necessity
These words have one *c* at the beginning, two *s*'s in the middle and the ending *-ary*.

negligence, negligent
Note that these have an *i* in the middle and the endings are *-ence*, *-ent*.

negligible
Take care to spell the ending of this word correctly; many people make the mistake of spelling it with *-able* at the end.
▶ *Spelling rule*: **-able, -ible**.

neighbour

This word has *-ei-* at the beginning, and the ending is *-our*. It is spelt with *-or* at the end in American English.

neither

This is spelt with *-ei-* at the beginning, not *-ie-* and so does not follow the normal spelling rule.

▶ *Spelling rule*: **i before e except after c**.

niece

The *-ie-* spelling of this word follows the normal rule.

▶ *Spelling rule*: **i before e except after c**.

ninth

The *e* is dropped from the word *nine* when forming this word.

noticeable

The final *e* is kept when adding the ending *-able* to *notice*, in order to preserve the soft *s* sound of the letter *c*.

▶ *Spelling rule*: **-able, -ible**.

> *Spelling Tip*
>
> The **ice** is not**ice**able.

nuisance

Note the *-ui-* at the beginning and the ending *-ance*.

nutritious

Note the *i* before the *-ous* at the end.

obscene, obscenity

Take care to remember the *-sc-* in the middle of these words.

occasion, occasional, occasionally

These words have two *c*'s and one *s*.

Spelling Tip

It's an **occa**sion for playing s**occ**er and **s**quash.

occupation, occupy
These words have two *c*'s and one *p*.

occur, occurred, occurring, occurrence
The *r* of *occur* is doubled when adding a suffix.
▶ *Spelling rule*: **Doubling final consonants**.

offence, offensive
The spelling is with a *c* in the noun *offence* (*He committed a serious offence.*) but is with an *s* for the adjective *offensive* (*I found the film quite offensive.*).

offered
You do not need to double the final *r* in *offer* when adding the ending *-ed*.
▶ *Spelling rule*: **Doubling final consonants**.

omit, omission
There is only one *m* in these words.

omitted, omitting
You should double the final *t* of *omit* when you add the endings *-ed* and *-ing*.
▶ *Spelling rule*: **Doubling final consonants**.

opponent
Note that this word has two *p*'s and one *n*. It may help to think of the related word *o**pp**osite*.

opportunity
This word has two *p*'s.

outrageous

Notice that the final *e* of *outrage* is kept before adding the ending -*ous* in order to preserve the soft *g* sound.

overrule

This word is formed from *over* and *rule*, hence the two *r*'s.

panicked, panicking, panicky

Words ending in -*c* usually add *k* before -*ed*, -*ing*, or -*y*.
▸ *Spelling rule*: **-c**.

paraffin

This has one *r* and two *f*'s. It may help to know that the person who discovered *paraffin* gave it this name because it has little chemical **affin**ity for other substances.

parallel, paralleled, paralleling

These words have one *r*, two *l*'s in the middle and one *l* at the end. Notice that the final *l* does not double before -*ed* and -*ing*.
▸ *Spelling rule*: **Doubling final consonants**.

> *Spelling Tip*
>
> a pai**r** of **l**ong **l**ines that **l**ie pa**r**a**l**le**l**

paralyse, paralysis, paralytic

These words have only one *r* and one *l*. *Paralyse* can only be written with an *s* in British English, never a *z*.

parliament, parliamentary

Remember the *i* between the *l* and the *a* in these words.

peaceable

The *e* of *peace* is retained to preserve the soft *s* sound of the *c* before the ending -*able*.
▸ *Spelling rule*: **-able, -ible**.

perennial
This word has only one *r* but two *n*'s, just as in the Latin phrase **per annum**.

permanent
Note that the spelling of the ending is *-ent*, not *-ant*.

> *Spelling Tip*
>
> a perman**ent** resid**ent**

permitted, permitting
The *t* of *permit* is doubled before adding *-ed* and *-ing*.
▸ *Spelling rule*: **Doubling final consonants**.

perseverance
Note the ending *-ance*.
▸ *Spelling rule*: **-ance, -ence**.

persistence, persistent
Note the endings *-ence* and *-ent*.
▸ *Spelling rule*: **-ance, -ence**.

Pharaoh
This is a word that causes difficulties for many people because of the ending *-aoh*.

> *Spelling Tip*
>
> **P**yramids **h**ouse **a**ncient **r**elics **a**nd **o**ther **h**istorical items belonging to the **Pharaoh**.

phenomenon
This is one of those words that sounds difficult to spell, but is actually quite simple, as long as you spell it exactly as it sounds, and remember the *ph-* at the beginning.

DIFFICULT WORDS

physically
Note the *ph-* and the *y*, and especially the *-ally*, which is simply *-ly* added to *physical*.

physique
The origins of this word are French, and this explains the spelling and the pronunciation of the *i* and the final *-que*.

picnicked, picnicker, picnicking
When a word ends in *c*, a *k* is usually added before a suffix beginning with a vowel, in order to preserve the hard *k* sound of the *c*.
▸ *Spelling rule*: **-c**.

picturesque
Note the *-que* ending of this word.

piece
The *-ie-* spelling follows the normal spelling rule.
▸ *Spelling rule*: ***i* before *e* except after *c***.

plateau
The plural can be plateaux or plateaus.
▸ *Spelling rule*: **plurals**.

plausible
Take care with the ending of this word, which is *-ible*, not *-able*.

playwright
This word is formed from *play* and *wright*, meaning 'a maker', as in *shipwright*. Don't be misled by the idea of 'writing'.

pneumonia
Take care to remember the silent *p* at the beginning.

Portuguese
Remember the *u* after the *g*.

possess, possession, possessive
This is a very possessive word and likes to own as many *s*'s as possible! All these words have two double *s*'s.

posthumous
Note the silent *h* in this word.

potato
This word is often mistakenly spelt with an *e* at the end. However, the plural *potatoes* does have an *e*.
▶ *Spelling rule*: **-os, -oes**.

precede
Note the ending is *-cede*, not *-ceed* as in *proceed*.
▶ *Spelling rule*: **-cede, -ceed, -sede**.

> *Spelling Tip*
>
> To pre**cede** is to be pla**ced** ah**e**ad.

predecessor
This word has one *c*, two *s*'s and the ending *-or*.
▶ *Spelling rule*: **-er, -or, -ar**.

preferable
This word has only one *r* and the ending is *-able*.
▶ *Spelling rule*: **-able, -ible**.

preference
Like *preferable*, this has only one *r*, but the ending is *-ence*. If in doubt, remember *preferential* when writing this word.

preferred, preferring
The final *r* of *prefer* is doubled before adding *-ed* and *-ing*.
▶ *Spelling rule*: **Doubling final consonants**.

DIFFICULT WORDS

preparation
Note the -*par*- in the middle of this word. It will help to remember the related words pre**par**e and pre**par**atory.

privilege
Many people find this word difficult to spell, the difficulty being the second syllable spelt with an *i*, and the ending -*ege* (not -*edge*). It may help to remember that pri***vile****ge* contains the word *vile*.

procedure
Note the single *e* of the second syllable.

proceed
Note the spelling of the ending -*ceed*.
▶ *Spelling rule*: **-cede, -ceed, -sede**.

profession, professional
These words have one *f* and two *s*'s.

professor
This word has one *f* and two *s*'s and the ending is -*or*.
▶ *Spelling rule*: **-er, -or, -ar**.

profitable, profited, profiting
There is only one *f* in the core word *profit*, and the final *t* does not double before adding a suffix.
▶ *Spelling rule*: **Doubling final consonants**.

pronunciation
Although this is related to the word *pronounce*, there is no *u* after the *n* and the word should be spelt as it sounds.

propellant
The *l* of *propel* is doubled before a suffix, and the ending is -*ant*.
▶ *Spelling rule*: **-ance, -ence**.

propeller
The *l* of *propel* is doubled before adding a suffix, and the ending is
-*er*.
▶ *Spelling rule*: **Doubling final consonants**.

protein
The -*ei*- spelling of this word goes against the normal spelling rule.
▶ *Spelling rule*: ***i* before *e* except after *c***.

psychiatry, psychiatrist, psychiatric, psychic, psychology, psychologist
The root of all these words is *psych*-, which means 'mind, soul'.

publicly
You may think that this word 'looks wrong', and this could be
because it is an exception to the rule for adding -*ly* to adjectives
ending in -*ic*.
▶ *Spelling rule*: **-ly**.

pursue
Note the spelling of the beginning part of this word, *pur*-.

pyjamas
Note the *y* in this word. It is spelt *pajamas* only in American
English.

> *Spelling Tip*
>
> **P**ut **y**our **py**jamas on.

questionnaire
All the words relating to the core word *question* have a single *n*
(*questioned*, *questionable*), except *questionnaire*, which has two.

queue
This is an unusual spelling, with a queue of *u*'s and *e*'s!

DIFFICULT WORDS

rebelled, rebelling, rebellion, rebellious
The *l* of *rebel* is doubled before adding a suffix.
▶ *Spelling rule*: **Doubling final consonants**.

recede
Note the ending *-cede*.
▶ *Spelling rule*: **-cede, -ceed, -sede**.

receipt
The *-ei-* in the middle of this word follows the normal spelling rule. Take care not to omit the silent *p* at the end.
▶ *Spelling rule*: ***i* before *e* except after *c***.

receive
The *-ei-* in the middle of this word follows the normal spelling rule.
▶ *Spelling rule*: ***i* before *e* except after *c***.

recognize
Be careful not to omit the *g*, which is often slurred in speech. This word may also be spelt with *-ise* at the end.
▶ *Spelling rule*: **-ise, -ize**.

recommend, recommendation
These words have only one *c* but two *m*'s.

reconnaissance
This has two *n*'s, two *s*'s and *-ance* at the end.

recurrence, recurrent
The final *r* of *recur* is doubled before adding a suffix beginning with a vowel, as in *occur*.
▶ *Spelling rule*: **Doubling final consonants**.

redundant, redundancy
Note the *-an-*. The plural of *redundancy* is *redundancies*.
▶ *Spelling rule*: **-y**.

referral, referred, referring
The final *r* of *refer* is doubled before adding *-al*, *-ed* and *-ing*, because the stress is on *-fer*.
▸ *Spelling rule*: **Doubling final consonants**.

refrigerator
Although there is a *d* in *fridge*, there is no *d* in *refrigerator*.

regretted, regretting, regrettable
The *t* of *regret* is doubled before an ending beginning with a vowel.
▸ *Spelling rule*: **Doubling final consonants**.

reign
Note the silent *g* in a king or queen's *reign*. It may help to know that this word comes from the Latin *regere*, 'to rule', in which the *g* would have been pronounced.

relevance, relevant
Note the *-lev-* of the second syllable, and *-an-* towards the end.

relief, relieve
The *-ie-* in this word follows the normal spelling rule.
▸ *Spelling rule*: ***i* before *e* except after *c***.

reminiscent
Note the *-min-* and the *-sc-* in this word.

remittance
Note the extra *t* when *-ance* is added to *remit*.
▸ *Spelling rule*: **Doubling final consonants**.

repetition, repetitive
Danger areas in these words are *-pet-* and *-it-*. However, these words act as spelling aids to each other, in that *-it-* is clearly pronounced in repet**it**ion, and *-pet-* in re**pet**itive.

reprieve

The -*ie*- in this word follows the normal spelling rule.

▸ *Spelling rule*: **i before e except after c**.

resemble, resemblance

Note the single *s* and the -*ance* ending.

▸ *Spelling rule*: **-ance, -ence**.

resign, resigned

Take care not to forget the silent *g* in these words. It will help to remember the related word *resignation*, in which the *g* is clearly pronounced.

resistance, resistant

Note the endings -*ance* and -*ant*.

▸ *Spelling rule*: **-ance, -ence**.

responsible

Note that the ending is -*ible*.

▸ *Spelling rule*: **-able, -ible**.

restaurant

The second syllable of this word is often slurred in speech, so take care not to omit the -*au*- when writing it. The word comes from French, originally *restaurer*, 'to restore', in this case, from hunger to fullness!

Spelling Tip

My **aunt** is in the rest**aura**nt.

retrieve

The -*ie*- in this word follows the normal spelling *rule*.

▸ *Spelling rule*: **i before e except after c**.

reversible

Note that the ending is -*ible*, not -*able*.

▸ *Spelling rule*: **-able, -ible**.

rhetoric, rhetorical, rhetorically
Take care not to omit the silent *h*.

rheumatism
Note the silent *h* and the position of the *e*.

rhinoceros
Note the silent *h* and the *c*.

rhubarb
Take care not to omit the silent *h*.

rhyme, **rhythm**
Both words begin with the same three letters, *rhy-*.

> *Spelling Tip*
>
> **R**emember **h**ow **y**ou begin **rhy**me and **rhy**thm.

ridiculous
Note the *i* of the first syllable. If in doubt, think of the related word *ridicule*.

righteous
Remember the *e* in this word, which turns the *t* sound at the end of *right* into the *ch* sound in *righteous*.

rigorous
The *u* of *rigour* is dropped before adding *-ous*.
▸*Spelling rule*: **-or, -our**.

riveting
You do not need to double the *t* of *rivet* when adding a suffix.
▸*Spelling rule*: **Doubling final consonants**.

saccharine

Note the double *c* and the *h*. The final *e* is optional when *saccharine* is used as a noun, but is obligatory in the adjective.

sacrilege, sacrilegious

Note the positions of the *i* and the *-eg-*. It may help to consider that this word is opposite in meaning to *religious*, and that the vowels *e* and *i* are the opposite way round too.

satellite

This has only one *t* but two *l*'s.

satisfactory

Note the *-ory* ending.

sceptic, sceptical

These words are spelt with *sc-*. *Skeptic(al)* is correct in American English.

schedule

Note the *sch-* spelling at the beginning.

scrupulous

This has one *p* and one *l*.

scythe

Note the *sc-* at the beginning.

secondary

Note that the ending is *-ary*, which is often slurred in speech.

secretary

The ending of this word is *-ary*. If in doubt, think of the related adjective *secretarial*.

seize, seizure
The spelling of these words is an exception to the normal spelling *rule*, so be particularly careful when writing them.
▶ *Spelling rule*: *i* **before** *e* **except after** *c*.

separable, separate, separation
Note the *-par-* spelling of these words. It may help to remember that people who are se**par**ate are a**part**.

sergeant
Everything between the *s* and the *t* in this word is a potential source of error! Note the *-er-*, the *-ge-* and the *-ant* ending.

sheikh
This comes from an Arabic word and does not follow the normal rules of English spelling. It can also be spelt without the final *h*.

siege
The *-ie-* in this word follows the normal spelling rule.
▶ *Spelling rule*: *i* **before** *e* **except after** *c*.

sieve
The *-ie-* in this word follows the normal spelling rule.
▶ *Spelling rule*: *i* **before** *e* **except after** *c*.

silhouette
Take care to remember the silent *h* in the middle of this word.

> *Spelling Tip*
>
> The **sil**ent **hou**se appeared in **silhou**ette.

sincerely
Note the *-cere-* in the middle of this word.

DIFFICULT WORDS

skilful, skilfully
One of the *l*'s of *skill* is dropped in *skilful*.
▶ *Spelling rule*: **-l, -ll**.

solemn
Take care to remember the silent *n* at the end of this word. It may help to think of the related word *solem**n**ity*.

somersault
This is not related to the word *summer*, but *summersault* is accepted by some as an alternative spelling.

sovereign, sovereignty
Take care when spelling this word, because the *-ei-* does not follow the normal spelling rule, the second *e* is often not pronounced in speech, and there is a silent *g*. It may help to remember that a sove**reign reign**s.
▶ *Spelling rule*: *i* **before** *e* **except after** *c*.

spaghetti
This has a silent *h* and double *t* at the end.

species
Note the *-ie-* in this word, which goes against the normal spelling rule.
▶ *Spelling rule*: *i* **before** *e* **except after** *c*.

speech
Note that the *ee* sound in this word is not spelt in the same way as the *ee* sound in *speak*.

stomach
Note the *o* and the *-ch*.

subterranean
See the note on **Mediterranean**.

subtle, subtlety, subtly
Note the silent *b* in these words and the spelling of *subtly*.
▶ *Spelling rule*: **-ly**.

> *Spelling Tip*
>
> Don't **subt**ract *b* from **subt**le!

succeed
This is spelt with double *c*, as the pronunciation would suggest, and ends in *-eed*.
▶ *Spelling rule*: **-cede, -ceed, -sede**.

success, succession, successive, successor
These words are all spelt with double *c*, as the pronunciation would suggest, and double *s*. Notice also the ending *-or* of *successor*.
▶ *Spelling rule*: **-er, -or, -ar**.

succinct
Note the double *c*, which the pronunciation would suggest.

succumb
Note the double *c* and the silent *b*.

superintendent
Note that the ending is *-ent*, not *-ant*.

supersede
This is the only word in English that ends in *-sede*.
▶ *Spelling rule*: **-cede, -ceed, -sede**.

supervise, supervisor
These words may not be written with a *z*. Note also the *-or* ending of *supervisor*.
▶ *Spelling rules*: **-ise, -ize** and **-er, -or, -ar**.

DIFFICULT WORDS

surprise, surprised, surprising
There are two *r*'s in these words; take care not to omit the first one!
These words can also never be written with a *z*.
▸ *Spelling rule*: **-ise, -ize**.

> *Spelling Tip*
>
> **U r** (you are) in for a su**r**prise.

susceptible
Note the *-sc-* and the ending *-ible*.
▸ *Spelling rule*: **-able, -ible**.

syringe
Note the position of the *y* and the *i*, often reversed in error.

tariff
This has one *r* and two *f*'s, like *sheriff*.

technique
Note the final *-que*.

televise
This may not be written with a *z*.
▸ *Spelling rule*: **-ise, -ize**.

temperamental
Take care not to omit the *-per-*, which is often slurred in speech.

temperature
Take care not to omit the *-per-*, which is often slurred in speech.

tendency
This word ends in *-ency*, not *-ancy*.

territory
Take care to remember the double *r*, and the ending *-ory*. It may help to think of the related word *territorial*.

thorough
Make sure you do not confuse the spelling of this word with *through*.

threshold
Although this word is often pronounced *thresh-hold*, there is in fact only one *h* in it.

tobacco, tobacconist
This has only one *b* and two *c*'s. If in doubt, think of the slang form of the word, *baccy*.

tomorrow
This has one *m* and two *r*'s.

tranquillizer, tranquillity
In British English, the *l* of *tranquil* is doubled, contrary to the general rule, before adding *-ize* and *-ity*. *Tranquilliser* (with an *s*) is also correct.
▶ *Spelling rules*: **Doubling final consonants** and **-ise, -ize**.

transferred, transferring, transferable
The final *r* of *transfer* is doubled when adding *-ed* and *-ing* because the stress is on the syllable *-fer*, but note that *transferable* is spelt with a single *r*.
▶ *Spelling rule*: **Doubling final consonants**.

transmitted, transmitter, transmitting
The final *t* of *transmit* is doubled when adding *-ed*, *-er* and *-ing*.
▶ *Spelling rule*: **Doubling final consonants**.

transparent
Note the ending *-ent*.

DIFFICULT WORDS

travelled, traveller, travelling
In British English, the final *l* of *travel* is doubled when adding *-ed*, *-er* and *-ing*.
▶ *Spelling rule*: **Doubling final consonants**.

truly
The *e* of *true* is dropped when adding *-ly*.
▶ *Spelling rule*: **-ly**.

turquoise
Note the *-qu-* in the middle of this word.

twelfth
Take care not to omit the *f*, which is often slurred or not pronounced in speech.

tyre
A car *tyre* is always spelt with a *y* in British English. In American English the spelling is *tire*.

underrate
This word is formed from *under* and *rate*, hence the double *r*.

unduly
The *e* of *due* is dropped before adding *-ly*, in *duly* and *unduly*.

unnatural
This word is formed from *un-* and *natural*, hence the double *n*.

unnecessary
This word is formed from *un-* and *necessary*, hence the double *n*.

unwieldy
Note the *-ie-* in the middle of this word, which follows the normal spelling rule.
▶ *Spelling rule*: *i* **before** *e* **except after** *c*.

> *Spelling Tip*
>
> Something un**wiel**dy **i**sn't **e**asily **l**ifted.

vaccinate
This has two *c*'s and one *n*.

vacuum
This has one *c* and double *u*.

valuable
The *e* is dropped from *value* before adding *-able*.

vanilla
This has one *n* and two *l*'s.

vegetable
Take care to remember the *e* of the second syllable. If in doubt, remember *veg*e*tation*.

vehicle
Remember the *h* in the middle, clearly pronounced in the related word *vehicular*.

verruca
This has two *r*'s and one *c*.

vigorous
Note that the *u* of *vigour* drops before adding *-ous*.
▶ *Spelling rule*: **-or, -our**.

villain
Take care not to write *villian* by mistake!

visitor
Note that the ending is *-or*.
▶ *Spelling rule*: **-er, -or, -ar**.

DIFFICULT WORDS

voluntary
Note the -*ary* ending, which is often slurred in speech.

Wednesday
The *d* in *Wednesday* is not always clearly pronounced in speech, so take care not to omit it.

weight
The spelling of this word does not follow the general rule. If in doubt, remember the spelling of **eig**ht.

weird
The spelling of this word does not follow the general rule and is spelt -*ei*- not -*ie*-.
▶ *Spelling rule*: **i before e except after c**.

whisky, whiskey
Both forms are correct, depending on where the drink originates from. Scotch *whisky* is spelt without the *e*, but Irish and American *whiskey* is spelt with the *e*. The plural of *whisky* is *whiskies*; the plural of *whiskey* is *whiskeys*.

wholly
The final *e* of *whole* is dropped before adding -*ly*, which goes against the general rule.
▶ *Spelling rule*: **-e**.

withhold
This word has a double *h*; it is formed from *with* and *hold*, both words being clearly pronounced in speech.

woollen, woolly
The final *l* of *wool* is doubled before adding -*y*.
▶ *Spelling rule*: **Doubling final consonants**.

worshipped, worshipper, worshipping

Note the double *p*'s, contrary to what you would expect from the general rule.

▶ *Spelling rule*: **Doubling final consonants**.

wrath

This has a very unusual spelling; take care with the silent *w* and the *a*.

> *Spelling Tip*
>
> He **w**as **r**eally **a**ngry – filled with **wra**th.

yacht

This word is spelt very differently from how it is pronounced so take extra care to remember the correct spelling.

yield

This follows the general rules of spelling.

▶ *Spelling rule*: *i* **before** *e* **except after** *c*.

yogurt, yoghurt

Both spellings are correct.

zealous

This is spelt in a very similar way to *jealous*. Take care to remember the -*ea*-.

> *Spelling Tip*
>
> A z**eal**ous person has **real** enthusiasm.

zigzagged, zigzagging

Note the double *g*'s, contrary to the general rule.

▶ *Spelling rule*: **Doubling final consonants**.

4 Confusable words

There are many words in the English language whose spellings are easily confused because they sound the same or are spelt in a similar way. This chapter lists the most common of these words, together with a brief explanation of how you can distinguish between them and spell them correctly. We also direct you to any relevant spelling rule covered in Chapter 2 in this book, where the points are treated in more detail. For some, we have even provided a tip to help you remember the correct spelling.

accede, exceed
These words sound very similar but have very different meanings. To *accede* to the throne is to become king or queen. To *accede* to something is to agree to it:

> *He acceded to my request.*

To *exceed* something such as an amount or a limit is to go beyond it:

> *His success exceeded all our expectations.*

accept, except
Accept is a verb meaning 'to take something that is offered to you'. It also means 'to believe or agree to something':

> *He accepted her kind offer of a lift home.*

> *We accept your account of what happened.*

Except means 'not including'. It is also used as a verb to mean 'leave out, exclude'.

Everyone except John got top marks.

I must except you from my criticisms.

> Spelling Tip
>
> It may help to remember that *except* is part of **except**ion and *accept* is part of **accept**ance.

access, excess

Access means 'right of way, approach, entry':

We gained access to the house through a window.

Less commonly, *access* can also mean 'a sudden attack or fit':

an access of rage

Excess means 'too much'. It can also mean 'an outrageous act':

Try not to eat to excess.

The press condemned the excesses of the soldiers.

adapter, adaptor

Both spellings are correct, but they have slightly different meanings. An *adapter* of something, such as a book, is someone who adapts it for a particular purpose:

the adapter of a novel for a television drama

An *adaptor* is a piece of equipment that can be attached to something else for a particular purpose:

If you don't have a spare socket, just use an adaptor.

addition, edition

An *addition* is something added on, or it can also refer to the act of adding:

a welcome addition to the family

I'm hopeless at addition.

An *edition* is a number of copies of a book, magazine or newspaper printed at one time, or a particular version of it. It can also be a single television or radio programme that is one of a series:

the evening edition of the newspaper

I don't have that particular edition.

Friday's edition of the breakfast programme.

advice, advise

To spell these words correctly, remember that *advice* is a noun, whereas *advise* is a verb:

She gave him some good advice.

I advised him to seek professional help.

▶ *Spelling rule*: **-ise, -ize**.

> Spelling Tip
>
> It may help if you remember that *ice* is a noun.

affect, effect

Affect is always a verb and has two main senses. The first is 'to influence, make a difference to':

The changes won't affect the staff in this branch.

The second is rather formal and means 'to pretend':

Although she affected ignorance, I think she knew more than she was letting on.

Effect can be a noun or a verb. As a noun it means 'result, consequence, impression':

What effect will these changes have on this branch?

As a verb it means 'to cause, bring about':

His aim was to effect a radical change in the party structure.

Spelling Tip

It may help to remember that *affect* and *alter* both begin with a.

aid, aide

Aid is help given to someone. It can be a noun or a verb:

We have pledged billions of pounds in aid.

efforts to aid stranded refugees

An *aide* is an assistant to someone who has an important job, especially in government:

A close aide to the minister refused to comment on the matter.

Spelling Tip

It may help to think that *aide* has an extra e, and an aide is an extra person to help someone.

allude, elude

To *allude* to something means to mention it in passing or in an indirect way:

She sometimes alluded to a long-lost step-brother living in Australia.

To *elude* something or someone means to avoid them or escape from them:

He had eluded capture for more than eight years.

Elude can also mean 'to be too difficult to understand, realize or remember' or 'to fail to obtain':

The appropriate word always seemed to elude him.

Sleep eluded her.

allusion

See **illusion**

altar, alter

Altar is a noun:

> *the high altar at Canterbury Cathedral*

Alter is a verb:

> *Little has altered in the village since the 60s.*

amend, emend

These words are often confused because the meanings are similar, the spellings are similar, and they sound the same. *Amend* is by far the most commonly used of the two and it means 'to alter, improve or correct something':

> *We shall amend the error as soon as possible.*

> *the amended version*

Amend is also used in the expression *make amends*:

> *He desperately wanted to make amends for ruining the evening.*

Emend is restricted to the context of writing or publishing, and means 'to correct the errors in' a piece of writing:

> *We will emend the manuscript where necessary.*

angel, angle

These words are pronounced differently. An *angel*, pronounced with a soft *j* sound, is a spiritual being believed by some to be a messenger of God:

> *The angels announced the birth of Christ.*

Don't confuse this with the word *angle*, pronounced with a hard *g* sound:

> *an angle of 90 degrees*

> *He angled the blinds to keep out the sun.*

annex, annexe

*An**nex***, stressed on the second syllable, is a verb meaning 'to add, attach, take possession of (a country or area of land)':

The former USSR annexed Latvia during the Second World War.

***An**nexe*, stressed on the first syllable, is a noun and can be spelt with or without the e, but the form with the e is more common:

The proprietor is planning to build an annexe onto the hotel.

artist, artiste

An *artist* is a person who paints pictures or is skilled in another of the fine arts, such as sculpture or music. In a more general sense, *artist* can be used to mean anyone who shows great skill in what they do:

a stained-glass artist

He's an artist with a fishing rod!

An *artiste* (pronounced ar-***teest***) is a performer in a theatre or circus or, less commonly, an actor:

a Parisian cabaret artiste

ascent, assent

The word *ascent* is to do with climbing or rising:

He led the first ascent of Everest.

the opposition's ascent to power

Assent is agreement, or to agree to something:

Both countries have given their assent to the treaty.

I assented to their request for more information.

aural

See **oral**

bail, bale

Bail is money that must be given to a court of law before an arrested person can be released while they are waiting for their trial, and if someone *is bailed*, they are released from custody by providing *bail*.

To *bail* or *bail out* also means to remove water from a boat or flooded place using a container. The spelling *bale* can also be used for this meaning, but is now less common than *bail*. *Bail out* also means 'to jump from an aircraft'.

A *bale* is a large quantity of something, such as hay, cloth or paper, tied in a bundle. This word can also be used as a verb:

The barn was filled with enormous bales of hay.

The hay has been cut and baled.

baited, bated

Bait is something used to trap or hook animals, and it can be a verb meaning to trap animals. Note the difference in spelling between *a baited trap* and the expression *with bated breath*.

bale

See **bail**

ballet, ballot

Ballet (pronounced **bal**-ay) is a type of dancing. A *ballot* is a method of voting.

base, bass

Base means 'basis, foundation, lowest point':

Line the base of the tin with greaseproof paper.

Bass is a musical term relating to the pitch of a voice or musical instrument:

He sings bass.

a bass guitar

bated
See **baited**

birth, berth
Birth means 'being born'. A *berth* is a bed on a train, boat or caravan, or a mooring place for a boat. *Berth* can also be used as a verb:

He booked a berth on the next ferry out.

The liner berthed at Liverpool.

bloc, block
A *bloc* is a group of nations, etc who have an interest or purpose in common:

the European trade bloc.

In all other senses, the correct spelling is *block*:

a block of flats

a chopping block

The truck blocked the road.

blond, blonde
The form *blond* is usually used to refer to men, and *blonde* to refer to women. Either form can be used to describe hair, but *blonde* is more common.

born, borne
Born can only be used in the passive construction of the sense 'to give birth to':

She was born of German parents.

Borne is the past participle of the verb *to bear*, both in the sense of 'to carry' and 'to give birth'.

He was borne shoulder-high after his victory.

She has borne him seven children.

bough, bow

Bough is a literary word meaning a branch of a tree. The *bow* of a boat is the front part of it; *bow* is also a verb meaning 'to bend at the waist'.

boy

See **buoy**

brake, break

Brakes are the controls in a vehicle that make it stop. *Brake* can be used as a verb meaning 'to slow down'. *Braked* is the only past form of the verb.

The brakes don't work properly.

She braked sharply at the traffic lights.

Break is a verb meaning 'to make something not work' or 'to smash into pieces'. It can also be a noun meaning 'a change of activity' or 'a short holiday'. *Broke* and *broken* are past forms of the verb.

They went to Prague for a weekend break.

I broke the cup.

She has broken her leg.

bridal, bridle

Bridal is an adjective describing things relating to a bride. A *bridle* is a horse's harness. *Bridle* is also a verb meaning 'to react angrily':

a bridal gown

He bridled at her insulting tone.

broach, brooch

To *broach* a subject means to bring it up, to start to talk about it. A *brooch* is an item of jewellery that can be pinned to clothing.

buoy, boy

Take care not to omit the *u* when referring to a *buoy* floating as a marker out at sea. *Buoy* is also used as a verb meaning 'to keep afloat', and figuratively, 'to keep up':

It's cruel to buoy up his hopes when he's unlikely to win.

canvas, canvass

Canvas is a strong fabric. *Canvass* is a verb meaning 'to ask for votes or support':

canvas shoes

canvassing for the Liberal Democrats

censer, censor, censure

A *censer* is a container in which incense is burnt, usually in a church. A *censor* is a person who examines books, letters or films and decides whether they contain any harmful material that makes them unsuitable for publication. *Censor* can be used as a verb:

His letter had been heavily censored.

Censure is criticism or blame. It can also be a verb:

A civil servant was censured for leaking the story to the press.

chord

See **cord**

cite, sight, site

To *cite* means 'to refer to' or 'to mention':

The company was cited in the court case.

A *sight* is something you see:

It was a sight for sore eyes.

A *site* is a place:

The site was flat and perfect for the structure.

coarse, course

Coarse is an adjective meaning 'rude, crude, rough'. *Course* is a noun meaning 'a series, route, etc', and a verb meaning 'to run':

> *coarse behaviour*

> *We were way off our course.*

> *Tears coursed down her cheeks.*

Note also the spelling of the expression *of course*.

comma, coma

A *comma* is a punctuation mark. A *coma* is a state of unconsciousness.

complacent, complaisant

Complacent means 'self-satisfied' or 'confident in your own abilities':

> *It's dangerous to get too complacent in today's cut-throat market.*

Complaisant (pronounced with a *z* sound) means 'willing to do what others want, especially in a cheerful, relaxed way':

> *Her father rarely allowed her to have her own way; it was her mother who was the complaisant one.*

complement, compliment

A *complement* is something that completes or perfects and can also be used as a verb meaning 'to enhance or complete':

> *A dry white wine is an ideal complement to fish.*

> *The curtains complemented the wallpaper.*

A *compliment* is an expression of praise or regard and can also be used as a verb meaning 'to praise':

> *My compliments to the chef.*

> *She was complimented on account of her good work.*

> *Spelling Tip*
>
> To **comple**ment means to **comple**te.

confidant(e), confident

A *confidant* is a man that you can confide in. The form with *e* is used for a woman:

Her sister is really her only confidante.

Confident is an adjective meaning 'having a strong belief in one's abilities, assured':

She was confident she would win.

cord, chord

Cord is the only correct spelling for the meaning 'string or cable' or 'ribbed fabric':

He tied the parcel with nylon cord.

trousers made of blue cord

Cord is now the usual spelling for the parts of the body known as the *vocal cords* and the *spinal cord*. In the musical and geometric senses, only *chord* is correct:

the opening chord of the sonata

A chord is a line joining any two points on a curve.

corps, corpse

A *corps* (pronounced *kor*) is a group of people working together or carrying out the same duties. A *corpse* (pronounced *korps*) is a dead body.

council, counsel

A *council* is a group of people who organize, control, take decisions or advise:

a council of ministers

Counsel is a rather formal word meaning 'advice', or it can mean 'a lawyer or lawyers':

> *his wise counsel*

> *counsel for the defence*

councillor, counsellor

A *councillor* is a member of a council. A *counsellor* is someone who gives advice.

course

See **coarse**

curb, kerb

A *curb* is something that holds someone back, restrains or controls. In British English, a *kerb* is the edging of the pavement. In American English this is also spelt *curb*.

currant, current

The spelling *currant* can only be used for the fruit. A *current* is a flow of air, water or electricity. *Current* is also an adjective meaning 'happening, being used or done at the present time'.

defuse, diffuse

To *defuse* a situation means to take the heat out of it:

> *He defused the argument by changing the subject.*

To *diffuse* something means to spread it out or disperse it:

> *The impact was diffused over a wide area.*

dependant, dependent

A *dependant* is someone who depends on another for money, food, etc:

> *As a young man without dependants, he was free to spend his money as he pleased.*

Dependent is an adjective meaning 'depending' (on):

He's still dependent on state benefits.

▸ *Spelling rule*: **-ance, -ence**.

desert, dessert

Deserts (pronounced *dez-*) are places where there is little rainfall. *Deserts* (pronounced *-zurts*) are 'things that a person deserves':

the Sahara Desert

He got his just deserts.

A *dessert* (pronounced *-zurt*) is a sweet dish served at the end of a meal:

We had apple pie for dessert.

> *Spelling Tip*
>
> **S**ugar and **s**pice are often found in a de**ss**ert.

device, devise

Device is a noun, and *devise* is a verb:

a device for boring holes

He devised a cunning plan.

Devise may not be spelt with a *z*.

▸ *Spelling rule*: **-ise, -ize**.

diffuse

See **defuse**

disc, disk

Disk is a computer term. The spelling *disc* is used in all other cases:

Please insert the floppy disk into the drive.

compact disc

discreet, discrete

Although these words come from the same Latin word, in English they are different words with different meanings. *Discreet* means 'not saying or doing anything that may cause trouble or embarrassment':

This is a very delicate matter: can we rely on you to be discreet?

Discrete means 'separate, not connected or attached to others':

We find that the pattern is formed from thousands of discrete dots of colour.

divers, diverse

Divers is an old, literary word meaning 'several'. *Diverse* means 'various, different'.

Mr Milton was relieved of a not inconsiderable quantity of gold coins and divers investments.

The shop sold a diverse range of gifts.

draft, draught

A *draft* is a rough sketch or outline, a bank order, or conscription into the army:

a rough draft of my speech

a bank draft for £5,000

He managed to avoid the draft because of his disability.

A *draught* is a current of air, a quantity of liquid, barrelled rather than bottled beer, and one of the pieces used in the game of draughts.

In American English, the usual spelling is *draft* for all the above senses.

dual, duel

Both these words are related to the idea of 'two'. *Dual* is an adjective meaning 'having two parts, functions'. A *duel* is a fight between two people. *Duel* can also be a verb meaning 'to fight':

a dual carriageway

duelling pistols

> Spelling Tip
>
> Du**a**l is an **a**djective.

dying, dyeing

Dying is a form of the verb *die*, and *dyeing* is a form of the verb *dye*:

Her plants are dying because she forgets to water them.

She's dyeing her hair blonde.

▶ *Spelling rule*: **-e**.

edition
See **addition**

effect
See **affect**

elicit, illicit

Elicit is a verb meaning 'to draw facts, a response, etc from somebody, often with difficulty':

I finally managed to elicit an answer from him.

Illicit is an adjective meaning 'unlawful' or 'not allowable':

illicit gambling activities

eligible, illegible

These words are sometimes confused in writing, possibly because they look similar, the initial *e* and *i* often being written the wrong way round. *Illegible* means 'not legible' and is formed from *legible*, plus the prefix *il-*:

The signature on the document is illegible.

Eligible means 'suitable, qualified, entitled':

> *You will not be eligible for this benefit if you work more than sixteen hours a week.*

elude
See **allude**

emend
See **amend**

emigrant
See **immigrant**

eminent, imminent
Eminent means 'outstanding, distinguished':

> *an eminent lawyer*

Imminent means 'about to happen'. It is often used in a negative context:

> *imminent job losses*

enquire, inquire
Some people think that *enquire* and *enquiry* should be used when simply asking about something, and that *inquire* and *inquiry* should be used for a more formal or detailed investigation into something. Many people however do not make this distinction, and it is not recognised by many authorities on English. In phrases such as *court of inquiry*, implying a detailed investigation, *inquiry* is the more usual spelling.

ensure
See **insure**

envelop, envelope
Envelop is a verb meaning 'to surround, cover', whereas an **envelope** is what you put a letter in:

The rich smell of the woods enveloped us.

an enveloping sense of happiness

exceed
See **accede**

except
See **accept**

excess
See **access**

exercise, exorcise
A good way to remember the two different spellings is to memorize this tip:

> *Spelling Tip*
>
> L**e**gs and p**e**ts are ex**e**rcised; gh**o**sts and sp**oo**ks are ex**o**rcised.

farther
See **further**

faze, phase
To *faze* means to confuse, shock or upset:

They were fazed by the size of the losses.

A *phase* is a period of time:

The campaign will comprise three phases.

flair, flare
A *flair* is a natural ability or cleverness:

She has a flair for languages.

A *flare* is something that burns or shines:

They lit flares when they heard the sound of the plane.

Flares are wide-bottomed trousers. *Flare* can also be used as a verb to mean 'to become wider':

The trousers flare slightly at the bottom.

floe, flow
A *floe* is a floating field of ice. For all other senses, the spelling is *flow*.

forego, forgo
To *forego* means to go in front of something:

It was a foregone conclusion.

To *forgo* means to go without something:

I think I will forgo the pudding.

▶ *Spelling rule:* **for-, fore-**.

further, farther
Further or *farther* is used when there is an actual physical distance involved, although *further* is now more common:

I can't walk any farther / further.

Further means 'additional' or 'beyond this point':

I would like to make one further point

Further is also used as a verb to mean 'to help to move towards success, completion, etc':

This will further his career prospects.

gamble, gambol
Lambs and children *gambol*; clients in a casino or betting shop *gamble*.

gaol, goal
Take care not to write *goal* when you mean *gaol* (*jail*).

gild, guild

To *gild* something means to cover it in gold. A *guild* is a society or association:

> *The picture frame had been gilded.*

> *a guild of master builders*

gilt, guilt

Gilt is the gold or gold-like material used for gilding. *Guilt* is shame or blame:

> *A bereaved person can sometimes experience feelings of guilt.*

goal

See **gaol**

gorilla, guerrilla

A *gorilla* is a very large ape. A *guerrilla* is someone who fights as part of an unofficial army. It may help to know that *guerrilla* comes from a Spanish word, *guerra*, meaning 'war'.

grill, grille

To *grill* is to cook food under direct heat, and a *grill* is the device for doing this, or food that has been *grilled*. A *grille* is a framework of bars over a window or door. This can also be spelt *grill*.

guild

See **gild**

guilt

See **gilt**

hail, hale

Hale is only used for the rather old-fashioned meaning, 'healthy', usually in the expression 'hale and hearty'. The spelling *hail* is used for all other senses of the word.

hangar, hanger

Aeroplanes are kept in *hangars*; clothes are hung on *hangers*. It may help to remember that there are two a's in **a**eropl**a**ne and **ha**ng**a**r.

hear, here

You use *hear* to talk about what your ears do.

> *Can you hear that noise?*

Here means 'in this place' or 'to this place'.

> *Do you live here?*

> *Spelling Tip*
>
> We h**ear** with our **ear**s.

hoard, horde

A *hoard* is a store or hidden stock of something. *Hoard* can also be used as a verb meaning 'to store, often secretly'. A *horde* is a crowd or a large number of people:

> *They've started to hoard tinned food and petrol.*
>
> *Hordes of tourists come here every year.*

idle, idol

Idle is an adjective meaning 'lazy, not working'. It can also be used as a verb:

> *idling away the hours*

An *idol* is something or someone worshipped like a god.

illicit

See **elicit**

illusion, allusion

An *allusion* is an indirect reference to something:

> *I understood this to be an allusion to his past life.*

An *illusion* is something that creates a misleading appearance or a false belief:

> *The high ceiling and white walls create the illusion of space in what is, in reality, quite a small room.*

immigrate, emigrate

To *immigrate* means 'to enter a country in order to live there'. A person who does this is called an *immigrant*, and the act of doing this is *immigration*:

> *There are many Irish immigrants in the USA.*

To *emigrate* means 'to leave a country in order to settle in another one'. A person who does this is called an *emigrant*, and the act of doing this is *emigration*:

> *Many Irish people have emigrated to the USA.*

> *Spelling Tip*
>
> The prefix *im-* is used with words beginning with *b*, *m* or *p* to mean 'into', hence **im**migration is *migration* into a country.

imminent
See **eminent**

inquire
See **enquire**

insure, ensure

To *insure* someone or something is to pay a sum of money in case of loss, injury or damage:

> *He insured his life for £100,000.*

To *ensure* that something happens means 'to make sure' that it happens:

> *Ensure you turn all the lights out when leaving the house.*

its, it's

Its means 'belonging to it'. It is part of the same family of words as *my*, *your*, *his*, *her*, *our* and *their*, called possessive pronouns:

> *The table was modern. Its legs were made of steel.*

It's is a contraction of 'it is' or 'it has':

> *It's lovely weather today.*

> *It's been ages since we last saw you.*

kerb

See **curb**

lead, led

Lead is the present tense of the verb *to lead*:

> *I lead from the front now – it's my new style.*

Led is the past tense of the verb *to lead*:

> *I led the meeting on the first three occasions; on the fourth, it was led by John.*

Lead is a metal:

> *She has shares in a lead mine.*

leant, lent

Leant is the past tense of the verb *to lean*.

> *He leant against the bar and asked for a pint.*

Lent is the past tense of the verb *to lend*.

> *I lent her the money for her flight.*

licence, license

Licence is the noun, and *license* is the verb. There is a *c* in the middle of both forms. In American English, *license* is used for the noun and the verb:

> *a driving licence*

licensed to drive a car

lightning, lightening
Lightning is a noun (it goes with thunder); *lightening* is the *-ing* form of the verb *lighten*.

> Spelling Tip
>
> Ligh**ten**ing something whi**ten**s it.

loathe, loath, loth
To *loathe* means 'to dislike. *Loath* or *loth* means 'unwilling':

The two women loathed each other.

He was loath/loth to give up his independence.

loose, lose
Loose (pronounced *loos*) is an adjective meaning 'not tight'; *lose* (pronounced *looz*) is a verb meaning to mislay:

a loose screw

She's worried she'll lose her job.

mat, matt, matte
There is no problem with the spelling of *mat* meaning 'a rug', but there can be some confusion in the spelling of the adjective, meaning 'dull, not glossy'. The usual spelling is *matt*, but *matte* is also used. The usual American English spelling for this meaning is *mat*, and this is also used in British English, but is quite uncommon:

a white matt emulsion for the walls

matte black

meat, meet, mete
Few people will make mistakes with the spelling of *meat*, meaning 'flesh' and *meet*, meaning 'to come together with'. There is however

an old or rather formal sense of *meet* that you may come across, meaning 'fitting, proper, suitable':

> *It is not meet that you should talk to one such as he.*

To *mete out* a punishment means to order that punishment:

> *The judge meted out severe sentences to all the accused.*

meter, metre

Metre is a unit of measurement; a *meter* is an instrument for measuring, such as a gas meter. In American English, *meter* is used for both senses.

miner, minor

A *miner* works in a mine. *Minor* is an adjective meaning 'lesser, less important'. A *minor* is also a young person who is not yet legally an adult.

Spelling Tip

A **mine**r works in a **mine**. **Minor** is related to **minor**ity.

moral, morale

Moral means 'relating to principles or beliefs about right and wrong'. It is also the correct spelling for the *moral* of a story. *Morale* is the amount of confidence and optimism someone has:

> *He seems to have no morals at all.*

> *In spite of the attacks, morale continues to be high among the troops.*

motive, motif

A *motive* is a reason for doing something. A *motif* is a pattern or a repeated design, theme or idea:

> *The police could not establish a motive for the crime.*

> *A motif running through the plot is guilt.*

naught
See **nought**

naval, navel
Naval means 'relating to the Navy'. Your *navel* is the small hollow in the centre of your abdomen. A *navel orange* is so called because it has a navel-like depression in the skin.

net, nett
Net is the more common form of this word, but in the 'profit' and 'weight' sense, *nett* is also correct, although not very common:

a fishing net

The net profit was £5,000.

350g nett weight

nougat, nugget
Nougat is a kind of sticky sweet, not to be confused with gold *nuggets*.

nought, naught
Nought and *naught* come from the same root word and their meanings are related, which is why some people confuse the spelling. *Nought* is zero, the number 0; *naught* means 'nothing' and is usually found in old-fashioned expressions such as *come to naught*.

nugget
See **nougat**

oral, aural
These are sometimes confused because they sound similar. *Aural* means 'relating to the ear', or 'listening'. *Oral* means 'relating to the mouth' or 'spoken':

an aural test

practising her accent for the oral part of the French exam

passed, past

Passed is the past form of the verb *pass*:

> *I passed him in the corridor.*

Past is the form you should use in all other senses of the word:

> *He stayed on past his stop.*
>
> *The ball whizzed past.*
>
> *our country's glorious past*

pastille, pastel

A *pastille* is a type of fruity sweet. *Pastels* are artists' crayons, or pictures drawn with them, hence also *pastel* colours.

pedal, peddle

You *pedal* a bicycle. To *peddle* goods means to sell them, often from door to door, or illegally.

> *Spelling Tip*
>
> A pe**dl**ar pe**ddl**es goods.

personnel, personal

Personnel is a noun meaning 'the people employed in a place of work'. Don't confuse this with the adjective *personal*, spelt with one *n* and an *a*:

> *Our personnel are highly trained.*
>
> *He will be making a personal appearance at the gala.*

phase

See **faze**

plane, plain

Plain is used mainly as an adjective meaning 'clear', 'honest', 'simple in design' or 'ordinary looking'. The only time when *plain* is used as a noun is for the sense 'a large flat area of land'.

Plane on the other hand is used mainly as a noun: it is an aeroplane, a type of tree, a tool for smoothing wood, a level or standard and a level surface in geometry. It can also be used as a verb to mean 'to glide smoothly' or 'to smooth a piece of wood'.

pore, pour

To *pore* means to examine closely:

She pored over the book, trying to find a mistake.

If you *pour* a liquid, you cause it to flow out:

He poured the wine into her glass.

practice, practise

To spell these words correctly, remember that *practice* is a noun and *practise* is a verb:

I went to tennis practice last night.

She practised her lines until she was word perfect.

Spelling Tip

It may help if you remember that *ice* is a noun.

pray
See **prey**

precede
See **proceed**

prey, pray

A bird or animal's *prey* is the creatures it hunts and kills for food. *Prey* can also be used as a verb:

These creatures are the prey of hawks.

The spiders prey on small insects.

To *pray* is to say a prayer.

principle, principal

These two words are one of the most frequently confused and misspelt pair of words in English. They have very different meanings.

Principal is an adjective as well as a noun. As an adjective, it means 'main' or 'most important':

> *He gave as the principal reason for his resignation lack of co-operation from colleagues.*

As a noun, it means 'person in charge':

> *Professor Hill took over as principal of the college.*

Principle is a noun meaning 'rule', 'theory' or 'moral guidelines':

> *the principles of English grammar*

> *I'm not going to sacrifice my principles for money.*

prise, prize

You *prise* open something that is difficult to open, usually with a tool. This can also, less commonly, be spelt *prize*:

> *I prised off the lid with the end of a spoon.*

You *prize* something valued and admired, such as someone's friendship. A *prize* is something won in a competition:

> *Her most prized possession is her collection of porcelain figurines.*

> *He got first prize in the 'best vegetable display' category.*

proceed, precede

Take care not to confuse *proceed*, meaning 'to go on or forward' with *precede*, meaning 'to go before'.

▶ *Spelling rule*: **-cede, -ceed, -sede**.

program, programme

In British English, *program* is only used for the computer science sense, and *programme* for all other senses. In American English, *program* is used for all meanings of the word.

The latest version of the program was downloaded from the Internet.

The training programme ensured they would continue their personal development.

prophecy, prophesy
Prophecy is the noun; *prophesy* is the verb.

quiet, quite
These words are not usually confused, but because they have the same letters, it is easy to make mistakes with your pen when writing or your fingers when typing!

raise
See **raze**

rapped, rapt, wrapped
Rapped and *wrapped* pose few problems, but note the spelling of *rapt*, meaning 'fascinated, attentive':

He listened to the speaker with rapt attention.

raze, raise
To *raze* is 'to destroy completely'. This can also be spelt *rase*, but this is uncommon. Take care not to confuse *raze* with *raise*, meaning 'to lift up', 'to increase':

The house was razed to the ground by fire.

The Bank of England has raised interest rates again.

reign, rein
A king or queen *reigns*; a horse has *reins*.

Spelling Tip

A kin**g** rei**g**ns.

review, revue

A *revue* is a type of light theatrical entertainment, usually about current events. A *review* is a report, study or critical consideration of something. It can be a noun or a verb:

> *She's performing in a revue at a local theatre.*

> *We'll review your progress at the end of the month.*

role, roll

Someone's *role* in something is the part they play in it. All other senses of this word are spelt *roll*:

> *The role of the monarchy has been seriously discredited.*

> *a bread roll*

> *His pen rolled under the table.*

sight, site

See **cite**

stanch, staunch

Stanch and *staunch* are both correct in the sense of 'stopping the flow of something', but *staunch* is by far the more common spelling. *Staunch* also means 'firm, trusty, steadfast':

> *efforts to staunch the oil spill*

> *a staunch supporter of the Communist party*

stationary, stationery

The spelling of these two words is often confused. *Stationary* is an adjective meaning 'not moving':

> *stationary traffic*

Stationery is a noun meaning 'writing materials':

a shop selling stationery

> Spelling Tip
>
> *Stationery* includes *writing pap**er***, and can be bought from a *station**er***; p**ar**ked c**ar**s are station**ar**y.

staunch
See **stanch**

stile
See **style**

story, storey
Storey and *story* can both be used to mean 'the floor or level in a building', but *story* tends to be used mainly in American English, *storey* being more usual in British English. Only *story* can be used for the meaning 'a tale, account of events':

an apartment block of fifty storeys

The story is set in and around a country hotel.

straight, strait
These words are sometimes confused. In most cases, you will probably need to use the spelling *straight*, meaning 'direct', 'not curved', 'clear', or 'conventional':

trying to get a straight answer from him

He described her as a very straight woman.

The common use of *strait* is the noun sense meaning 'a narrow strip of sea between two pieces of land':

the Straits of Gibraltar

CONFUSABLE WORDS

Straits in the plural is used to mean 'difficulty' or 'need':

> *She found herself in dire straits.*

> *desperate financial straits*

Strait is also an old adjective, meaning 'narrow', 'confined' or 'confining' and can now be found in compound words like *straitjacket* and *strait-laced*.

sty, stye

Pigs live in a *sty*. A *stye* or *sty* is a swelling on the eyelid.

style, stile

Style is elegance, or a particular way of doing or presenting something. A *stile* is a set of steps on either side of a fence or wall.

swat, swot

To *swat* something such as an insect means to hit it. *Swot* is an informal word meaning 'to study'. A *swot* is someone who studies a lot, probably too much:

> *swatting flies with a magazine*

> *He spent all summer swotting for his exams.*

there, their, they're

There means 'at, in, or to that place':

> *There they can do as they please; it is their retreat from the world.*

Their means 'belonging to them':

> *They can do what they like in their own home.*

They're is short for 'they are'. The apostrophe indicates where the missing a would have been:

> *They're moving their desks over there.*

theirs, there's

Theirs is part of a group of words consisting of *mine*, *yours*, *his*, *hers*, *its*, *ours* and *theirs*. *There's* is short for 'there is' or 'there has'. The apostrophe indicates where the missing *i* or *ha-* would have been:

> *We can put ours here and they can put theirs over there.*

> *The traffic's bad because there's been an accident.*

through, though

These words are not usually confused, but because their spellings are very similar, it is easy to make mistakes with your pen when writing or your fingers when typing!

tire, tyre

Tire is a verb meaning 'to become, or cause to become tired'. This is sometimes confused with the spelling of the word for the thick rubber strip round a wheel, because although this is spelt *tyre* in British English, it is spelt *tire* in American English.

to, too, two

These words all sound alike, but are spelt differently. *To* is the most common:

> *going to the shops*

> *pulled the door to*

Too means 'more than is needed or wanted' and 'also':

> *It's far too hot to do anything today.*

> *You can come along too.*

Two is the number that follows one:

two o'clock

dinner for two

> **Spelling Tip**
>
> It may help to think that **too** has **too** many o's, or is spelt
> **t** plus **o**, and **also** another **o**.

troop, troupe

A *troop* of people or some animals is a group of them:

a troop of scouts

a troop of monkeys

Troupe is used for a group of performers:

a troupe of acrobats

tyre

See **tire**

vain, vein

Vain is an adjective meaning 'proud of one's looks'. A *vein* is a
channel, like the veins in the body:

He's superficial, vain and frankly, quite irritating.

They struck a rich and deep vein of gold.

waive, wave

To *waive* a right or a rule means to give it up or abandon it:

He waived his claim to the land.

They waive admission charges on bank holidays.

All other senses are spelt *wave*:

60-foot-high waves

a crime wave

waving goodbye to his chance of fame

where, we're, were, wear

Where relates to place:

> *Where did you leave the papers?*

We're is short for 'we are'. The apostrophe indicates where the missing *a* would have been:

> *We're going to be late.*

Were is a form of the verb *be*, used when talking about the past:

> *The children were very excited.*

Wear means 'be dressed in':

> *What shall I wear tomorrow?*

Spelling Tip

It may help to think that w**here** relates to **here**, in meaning and spelling.

---

whose, who's

Whose should be used to mean 'of whom' or 'of which':

> *the boy whose father is a policeman*

> *the book whose pages are torn*

Who's is short for *who is* or *who has*. The apostrophe indicates where the missing *i* or *ha-* would have been:

> *Who's there?*

> *I'm looking for the person who's taken my pen.*

wrapped

See **rapped**

CONFUSABLE WORDS

yoke, yolk

A *yoke* is a burden, and it can be a verb meaning 'to join'. *Yolk* is the yellow part of an egg:

Many people are still suffering under the yoke of poverty.

yoked together in marriage

your, you're

Your means 'belonging to you' and is part of the group of words that includes *my*, *his*, *her*, *our*, *its* and *their*:

Are those your CDs?

You're is short for *you are*. The apostrophe indicates where the missing *a* would have been:

Come on, Isobel, you're next.

5 Building words with prefixes and suffixes

Prefixes and suffixes are groups of letters added to words or roots of words to create new words. (A root word stands on its own as a word but can be added to.) Prefixes and suffixes were originally words in their own right, usually from other languages, but over time they have been incorporated into English to modify or extend the meanings of root words, or to create new words. Learning the meanings of prefixes and suffixes can help you spell a word correctly. For example, knowing that the prefix *bi-* means 'two' will help you spell *bicycle*, a cycle with two wheels, or *biannual*, happening two times a year. Similarly, knowing that the suffix *-ward* means 'in the direction of' will help you spell words like *eastward* and *downward*.

Prefixes

Prefixes are groups of letters placed before words or roots of words. Every prefix has a meaning. Even the word prefix has a prefix in it: *pre-* meaning 'before', which has been added to *fix*, meaning 'to fasten'. Generally, when you add a prefix to a root word, the spelling of the prefix and the root word stays the same:

mis-	+ *fire*	= *misfire*
im-	+ *mature*	= *immature*

An exception is the prefix all- in which the final l is dropped when it is added to a word:

all-	+ *together*	= *altogether*
all-	+ *ways*	= *always*

BUILDING WORDS WITH PREFIXES AND SUFFIXES

You can add more than one prefix to a word:

re-   + *dis-*   + *cover*   = *rediscover*

And you can add prefixes to a word that has already had a suffix added to it:

re-   + *play*   + *-ing*   = *replaying*

The following is a list of common prefixes, with a brief explanation of what they mean, together with examples:

Prefix	Explanation	Example
a-, *an-*	without, not	asexual, amoral, anarchy, anhydrous, Anabaptist, anachronism
ab-	away, from, off	absent, abnormal, abduct
ad-	toward, make, against	adhere, admit, adumbrate
amphi-, *ambi-*	around, both sides	amphitheatre, ambidextrous, ambivalent
ante-	before	anteroom, antecedent
anthropo-	man	anthropology
anti-	against	antibiotic, antitank
aqua-	water	aquarium, aquarobics
audio-	hear	audiotypist, audiovisual
auto-	self	autograph, autobiography, automatic
bi-	two	bicycle, biannual, bisexual
bio-	life	biology, biorhythm, biosphere
circum-	around	circumference, circumnavigate
co-	together	co-operate, coenzyme

com-	with, together, in association	combine, commemorate, commiserate
de-	separation, away, opposite of, reduce	decouple, depart, deactivate, decrease
di-	two, double	dialogue, diarchy, dimorphism
dis-	opposite, apart, away, not	disagree, disperse, disinherit
ego-	self	egocentric, egomania
en-	cause to be, put in or on	enclose, envelope
epi-	upon, over	epidermis, epidemic
ex-	from, out of, apart, away	exhale, exterior, extraneous
geo-	earth	geography, geology, geocentric
graph-	write, record	graphics, graphology
hetero-	mixed, unlike	heterosexual
homo-	same, alike	homogenous, homosexual
hydro-	water	hydrant, hydroelectricity, hydrofoil
hypo-	under, inadequate	hypoallergenic, hypochondriac, hypocrisy
hyper-	over, excessive	hyperactive, hypermarket, hypertension
ideo-	idea	ideology, ideal
il-	not	illogical, illiterate
im-	not	impossible, immoral

BUILDING WORDS WITH PREFIXES AND SUFFIXES

in-	not, the opposite, the reverse	injustice, incredible
in-	into, in, within	inhale, incorporate, incarcerate
inter-	between	international, intergalactic, interact
ir-	not	irresolute, irresponsible
macro-	great, long	macrobiotic, macroeconomics
micro-	small	microfilm, microscope
mis-	wrongly, badly	misbehave, mismanage
mono-	single	monocle, monogamy
pater-	father	paternal, paternity
ped-	foot	pedal, pedestrian, pedicure
peri-	around	perimeter, peripatetic, periscope
phil-	love	philanthropy, philosophy
poly-	many	polygamy, polyphonic
post-	after	posterior, postnatal, postscript
pre-	before	preschool, preview, pre-war
pro-	before, in favour of	proceed, proactive, projection
psycho-	soul, mind	psychiatric, psychoanalyse, psychology
re-	again	recapture, revisit
sub-	under	submarine, subterfuge, subtle
super-	above, beyond, greater	superfluous, superhero, supervisor
syn-	with	synchronize, synod, synthesis

tele-	distant	telecommunication, teleconference
trans-	across	transport, transcend, transsexual
un-	not	unattractive, unnecessary, unplanned

Suffixes

Suffixes are groups of letters placed at the ends of words. Adding suffixes to words can change or add to their meaning. For example, adding the suffix *-hood* to *adult*, will create a new word, *adulthood*. Suffixes are also added to words to show how a word will be used in a sentence and what part of speech (noun, verb, adjective, etc) the word belongs to. For example, if you want to use the root word *talk* in a sentence, you may need to add the suffix *-s*, *-ing* or *-ed* to indicate when the action occurred or who was doing the action:

*I had been talk**ing** to Julie when the phone rang.*

*He talk**s** an awful lot.*

Sometimes, when you add a suffix to a root word, the spelling of the suffix and the root word stays the same:

| *help* | + *-ful* | = *helpful* |
| *accept* | + *-able* | = *acceptable* |

However, in many cases the spelling of the root word changes:

ease	+ *-y*	= *easy*
happy	+ *-ness*	= *happiness*
travel	+ *-ed*	= *travelled*

A comprehensive list of spelling rules explaining these changes in spelling can be found in Chapter 2.

As with prefixes, you can add more than one suffix to a root word:

| hope | + -ful | + -ly | = hopefully |

And you can add suffixes to a word that has already had a prefix added to it:

| un- | | + necessary | + -ly | = unnecessarily |

The following is a list of common suffixes, with a brief explanation of what they mean, together with some examples:

Suffix	Explanation	Example
-able, -ible	able, capable	breakable, debatable, lovable
-ade	result of an action	blockade
-age	act, state, result of	damage, storage, wreckage
-al	relating to	manual, natural, usual
-algia	pain	neuralgia, nostalgia
-an, -ian	native of, relating to	American, Georgian, thespian
-ance, -ancy	action, process, state	assistance, allowance, defiance
-ation	quality or act of	admiration, examination
-cian	skill or art of	magician, optician
-cy	action, function of	captaincy, hesitancy
-cide	killing	germicide, homicide, suicide
-cracy	rule	autocracy, bureaucracy, democracy
-dom	quality, realm	freedom, kingdom
-ee	receiver of	employee, lessee, refugee
-en	made of	silken, woollen

-ence, -ency	action, state, quality	agency, confidence, urgency
-er, -or	one who, that which	baker, instructor, fastener
-ese	native to, the language of	Chinese, Maltese
-ess	female of	baroness, lioness
-fic	making, causing	scientific, specific
-ful	full of	careful, hopeful, painful
-fy	make	liquefy, magnify, purify
-hood	quality, condition	childhood, widowhood
-ic, -ical	like, in the nature of	atomic, biological, poetic
-ion	act, result, state of	corruption, exhaustion, oppression
-ish	resembling	faddish, whitish
-ism	manner, condition, system	alcoholism, Catholicism, mannerism
-ist	one who	optometrist, florist
-ity, -ty	state of, quality	cruelty, oddity, purity
-ive	causing	abortive, exhaustive
-ize, -ise	make	Americanize, legalize, popularize
-logy	study, science of	meteorology, pathology
-less	without	careless, painless, thoughtless

BUILDING WORDS WITH PREFIXES AND SUFFIXES

-ly	like, in that manner	easily, mainly, quickly
-ment	act, state or result of	amazement, payment, retirement
-ness	state of	darkness, deafness, kindness
-oid	resembling	anthropoid, rhomboid
-ous	full of	humorous, odoriferous
-ship	state of, office	companionship, governorship
-some	like, apt	fulsome, wholesome
-tude	state, condition	aptitude, solitude
-ward	motion in the direction of	downward, homeward
-y	resembling, inclined to	bushy, panicky

6 American spelling

There are a number of minor differences between British English and American English spelling, the most important of which are listed here.

Doubling consonants

In British English, when the endings *-ing*, *-ed* and *-or/-er* are added to verbs ending in *l* and *p*, the *l* and *p* are doubled:

travel → travelling   equal → equalled

worship → worshipping   kidnap → kidnapper

In American English, they are not doubled:

travel → traveling   equal → equaled

worship → worshiping   kidnap → kidnaper

This difference also applies to certain nouns and adjectives:

British English	American English
woollen	*woolen*
carburettor	*carburetor*

It is worth noting that the British spellings are exceptions to the doubling rule described on page 28. The American spellings agree with the rule.

-ize and -ise

When British spelling allows verbs to end either in *-ize* or *-ise*, the spelling is always *-ize* in American English:

British English	American English
characterize or *characterise*	*characterize*
realize or *realise*	*realize*
apologize or *apologise*	*apologize*

American spelling also uses *-yze* where British spelling uses *-yse*:

British English	American English
analyse	*analyze*
breathalyse	*breathalyze*

-our and -or

Most words that end in *-our* in British English end in *-or* in American English:

British English	American English
colour	*color*
humour	*humor*
neighbour	*neighbor*
rumour	*rumor*
flavour	*flavor*
honour	*honor*

-re and -er

Many words that end in *-re* in British English end in *-er* in American English:

British English	American English
centre	*center*
theatre	*theater*
fibre	*fiber*
spectre	*specter*
meagre	*meager*
metre	*meter*

⚠️ **Warning:** Most words that end in -cre or -gre are exceptions to this: *acre*, *massacre* and *ogre* are spelt the same way in both British and American English.

-oe- and -ae-

Words that come from Latin and Greek and are spelt with -oe- and -ae- in British English, tend to be spelt with just an *e* in American English:

British English	American English
foetus	*fetus*
diarrhoea	*diarrhea*
oesophagus	*esophagus*
anaesthetic	*anesthetic*
anaemia	*anemia*
paediatric	*pediatric*

Note however that *fetus* is also the approved British spelling in scientific writing, and that *encyclopedia* and *medieval* are now more common in British English than *encyclopaedia* and *mediaeval*.

-ogue and -og

Most words spelt -ogue in British English are spelt -og in American English:

British English	American English
dialogue	*dialog*
prologue	*prolog*
catalogue	*catalog*
analogue	*analog*
epilogue	*epilog*
monologue	*monolog*

-l and -ll

Some words that end in a stressed vowel followed by *l* in British English have the *l* doubled in American English:

British English	American English
enrol	*enroll*
fulfil	*fulfill*
enthral	*enthrall*

See also the spelling rule on page 40.

-nce and -nse
Nouns that end in *-nce* in British English are spelt *-nse* in American English:

British English	American English
defence	*defense*
licence	*license*
offence	*offense*
pretence	*pretense*

Other words spelt differently in American English
Here is a short list of other common words spelt differently in American English:

British English	American English
aeroplane	*airplane*
annexe	*annex*
axe	*ax*
cheque	*check*
doughnut	*donut*
draught	*draft*
gauge	*gage*
grey	*gray*
jewellery	*jewelry*
kerb	*curb*
mould	*mold*
moult	*molt*

liquorice	*licorice*
plough	*plow*
practise (verb)	*practice*
programme	*program*
pyjamas	*pajamas*
sceptic	*skeptic*
skilful	*skillful*
storey	*story*
sulphur	*sulfur*
tyre	*tire*
vice (= the tool)	*vise*

7 Tips for improving your spelling

Many words in the English language are difficult to spell because they do not fit any of the spelling rules, are exceptions to those spelling rules, come from other languages that have completely different spelling rules to English, or are easily confused with other, similar words. In this chapter we give you some helpful tips and strategies to help you improve your spelling. The chapter is divided into three sections: specific techniques for learning difficult spellings; general spelling strategies; and checking that you have spelt a word correctly.

Techniques for learning difficult words

Sounding out the letters
Some words are easiest to spell by sounding out the individual sounds that each letter or group of letters produces, as in *d-i-a-r-y*. Sometimes it may be helpful to break the word down into separate syllables, for example *re-spon-si-bil-i-ty*. Many people find that mentally sounding out a difficult word and learning the sounds, rather than the combination of letters, helps them spell a difficult word. For example, mentally saying *mer-ing-you* may help you spell the word *meringue* correctly.

Finding words within words
Many tricky words have other, unrelated, words inside them, or at the beginning or end. For example, the word *favourite* contains *our* and *rite*, the word *definitely* has the word *finite* in it, and *across* has the word *cross* in it. Finding and remembering these words within words can help you to learn a difficult spelling. The words-within-words strategy can be particularly useful for remembering the

spelling of unstressed or silent vowels, for example *get* in *vegetable* or *sin* in *business*.

Visualization and shapes

You can use the shape or sound of the letters in a word to help you picture the word in your mind. For example, you can remember the two *i*'s of *definite* by seeing them as two eyes on either side of the *n* (the nose). Another word that can be visualized is *rhinoceros* (the silent *h* is like the horn on its head).

If you are asked to spell something, and you are unsure of the spelling, you will probably reach for a pen and write the word down – possibly in more than one way. You will then select the one that 'looks right'. This is a completely logical and natural method for identifying a correct spelling, because the eyes play a very important part in spelling, far more important in fact than the ears. If you can look at your own writing and tell which words 'don't look right', then you are half way to becoming a good speller.

Another method of remembering the spellings of words through visualization is to think about the shape of a word by imagining drawing a line around its outline. This is in fact one of the ways children first learn to read, so you will simply be using a skill that has been dormant for many years! Does the word have a lot of tall letters? Is the word long or short? Does it have many letters that descend below the line? This makes what is a called a 'spelling silhouette' and can help you to decide if the word looks right when you write it down yourself.

Mnemonics

A mnemonic (pronounced *ni-**mon**-ik*) is a rhyme or guide that helps you to remember something. For example, a well-known mnemonic for helping to remember the points of the compass clockwise is 'Naughty Elephants Squirt Water' (North, East, South, West). Many people find mnemonics to be a useful tool for helping them to remember the spelling of difficult words.

TIPS FOR IMPROVING YOUR SPELLING

The best mnemonics are short, simple and catchy, and are especially memorable if they make you smile! For example, an amusing mnemonic for remembering the spelling of *assassination* is '**assassination** involves two **ass**es and one **nation**'. A mnemonic should create a vivid image in your mind associated with the word you are trying to spell. In Chapter 3 of this book, we provide mnemonics for some of the more difficult words that don't follow spelling rules, or cannot easily be remembered using other methods, but the most helpful mnemonics will always be the ones you invent yourself.

Look, cover, write, check

This is a simple four-stage method for learning difficult spellings. Firstly, look at the word, then cover it over and write it down from memory, then uncover it to check that you have spelt it correctly. When you first look at the word, or if you get the spelling wrong, concentrate on the parts that you have problems with, or that are not spelt as they sound. Repeat the process until you are confident that you have learnt the correct spelling.

General spelling strategies

Spelling rules

Spelling rules can help you understand what often seems to be a complete lack of logic in the way a word is spelt. For example, why is the final letter of some words doubled when adding a suffix like *-ing* but not others? The *r* at the end of *refer* is doubled when you add the endings *-ed* or *-ing* (*referred*, *referring*), but the *r* at the end of *enter* is not (*entered*, *entering*). The answer in this case is that one of the criteria for doubling a final consonant is that the stress of the word must be on the final syllable, and in *en**ter*** the stress is on the first syllable.

Whilst you may not need to learn all the spelling rules of English – and indeed this would be quite an arduous task – knowing about and understanding them will help you to spell certain words with much more confidence. Chapter 2 of this book lists the main spelling rules, together with some common exceptions.

Root words, prefixes and suffixes

A root word stands on its own as a word but can be added to. Prefixes and suffixes are groups of letters added to words or to roots of words to modify or extend their meanings or to create new words. Prefixes are placed before words or roots of words, and suffixes are added at the ends of words. When trying to spell a difficult word, you may find it helpful to look for any root or core word within the word you are trying to spell, and identify any prefixes and suffixes added to it.

Many words in English can be broken down into known roots, with or without prefixes and suffixes. For example, the core or root of the word *commemorate* is the same as that of *memory* and *memorial*, to which the prefix *com-* has been added. Some words will consist of a root word, plus several prefixes or suffixes, for example *in-defens-ible*.

Learning the meanings of prefixes and suffixes can help you spell a word correctly. For example, the prefix *hyper-* means 'over', 'excessive', so this will help you spell the beginning of words like *hypermarket* and *hyperactive*; the suffix *-cracy* means 'rule', so this will help you spell the ending of the word *democracy*. Chapter 6 of this book lists the main prefixes and suffixes used in English, together with their meanings.

Finding letter patterns

Sometimes it can help to identify letter patterns in groups of words and use similar letter patterns or features from words you do know how to spell to help you spell others. For example, *conscience* and *conscientious* both have the pattern of letters *-scien-* in the middle, and the letters *chron-*, from the Greek word *chronos*, meaning 'time' will help you spell words like *chronicle*, *chronology*, *chronometer* and *synchronize*.

Word webs

A word web is a diagram showing how one word may be linked to several other groups of words. For example, the word *insignificant* can be linked to words with the prefix *in-*:

inedible   *informal*

It can also be linked to words with the suffix *-ant*:

arrogant   *buoyant*

And with words containing the root *sign*:

signature   *designer*

It can be linked to words related to *significant*:

significance   *signify*

Sometimes the word web has a short root word at the centre:

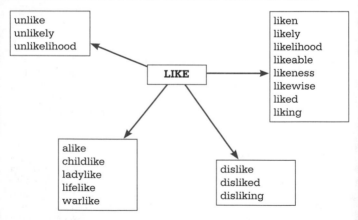

Narratives

One way to remember lists of words that have the same letter pattern, or the same spelling problem, is to make up a short narrative containing as many of the words as possible. For example, the following passage contains ten words ending in -o that have the plural -oes:

> *Ships carrying cargoes of potatoes and tomatoes were wrecked by tornadoes and enemy torpedoes. The sailors swam to an island where buffaloes roamed the slopes of volcanoes and where they were treated as heroes. They ate mangoes all day in caves full of echoes.*

If you are wondering how to spell the plural of a word that ends in -o, remembering this story might help you.

Checking your spelling

Spellcheckers

Computer spellcheckers are a useful way of checking your spelling and picking up mistakes. However, you should also be aware of their limitations:

- They can only check for incorrect spellings, so they will not tell you if you have used the wrong homophone – that is, words that sound alike but are spelt differently. For example, they cannot differentiate between *there* and *their*, because there is not a misspelling, just the wrong word in the wrong place. For the same reason, they will not tell you if you have accidentally typed the wrong word, for example *that* instead of *than*.
- The list of words that the computer checks against does not contain every word in the English language. Some correctly spelt words may be marked as wrong, simply because they are not on its list. However, you can customize the dictionary on your computer and add missing word for future spelling checks.

You should also make sure that the language is set to British English rather than American English, or the checker will tell you that words like *theatre* are incorrect.

TIPS FOR IMPROVING YOUR SPELLING

Using dictionaries

Before the advent of spellcheckers, dictionaries were traditionally used to check the spellings of words, as well as for finding out definitions of words. We have seen that spellcheckers have their limitations, but a comprehensive, up-to-date dictionary will always give you the correct, contemporary spelling of a word.

There are ways to speed up how quickly you can find the word you want in a dictionary. Think of the dictionary as having four parts (quartiles), approximately A–D, E–L, M–R and S–Z. So if you are looking for the word *catapult*, open the dictionary in the first quartile; if you are looking for *mysterious*, open it just past the middle. Also, in any two-page spread of a dictionary, the first word on the left-hand page will also be printed in the top left-hand corner of the left page, and the last word on the right-hand page will also be printed in the top right-hand corner of the right page.

Some dictionaries will put words with suffixes at the end of the entry for the word they are derived from, rather than giving every single word an entry of its own. So if you are looking for *efficiency*, for example, you may not find it above *efficient* (where you might expect it to be), but at the end of the entry for *efficient*, along with *efficiently*. Some dictionaries also may not list all the words with a prefix that could be used to form an infinite number of words, for example the prefix *un-*. It will only list the most common, so you may have to go to the entry for the word without the prefix.

One problem is of course finding a word in a dictionary when you do not know how to spell it in the first place or are not sure that you have spelt the word correctly. For example, unless you are aware that there is a silent *p* at the beginning of *pterodactyl* or *psychopath*, you will have a long and fruitless search for the correct spelling under *t* or *s*. Even where there are no silent letters to complicate matters, the rules of spelling will often allow several possible spellings of a word, not all of which would necessarily occur to you. It would, for example, be pointless searching for *fascist* under *fash-* or *diarrhoea* under *diare-*.

To help with this difficulty, this book provides a list of alternative spellings for various English sounds. If you have searched for a word in a dictionary and failed to find it where you expected it to be, check the list on pages 176–182 and try looking under some of the spellings suggested there.

Proofreading your work

It is always good practice to proofread what you have written, however good you think are at spelling. Although we all make mistakes, we also tend to be very unforgiving of others' mistakes, and in some environments, our professional reputation could be at stake for want of a missing letter! Unfortunately, after all the time and effort that goes into writing something, it can be a real chore to proofread properly, and often this ends up as a very quick glance over the text. You might find it helpful to leave what you have written for a few hours before proofreading, and go back to it later. This means you will look at it with a fresher eye; you will be surprised at the errors you miss when you are over-familiar with the text.

When proofreading, it is important that you read each word slowly and carefully. One method of ensuring that you do this is to place a ruler under the line you are reading and, even better, point to each word as you read it, paying particular attention to words such as homophones (words that sound alike but are spelt differently). You may sometimes find it useful to cover half of a long word with your finger while you read the other half, or to read it syllable by syllable to make sure there are no letters missing, for example *artifical* for *artificial* or *accomodate* for *accommodate*. Another useful tip is to print off what you have written; you are more likely to spot errors on hard copy than on electronic versions.

Finding a word you cannot spell

Sometimes it is difficult to find a word in a dictionary or a book such as this when you cannot spell it in the first place. This appendix contains a list of different spellings for various English sounds. If you cannot find a word in a dictionary or other list, pick out the sound you are looking for in this list and try looking again under one of the other spellings.

Sound	Possible spelling	Examples
a	a	hat, castle, path
	au	laugh, draught
	ai	plaid
	i	meringue
ah	al	half, calf
	ar	part
	ea	heart
	er	clerk, sergeant
	aa	bazaar
aw	aw	draw
	or	order, sport
	ou	brought
	au	caught
	oa	broad
	oor	floor
	ore	bore
	our	four, tour
	ure	pure
ay	ay	pay
	ai	paid, straight

	a-e	make, age
	ea	break
	ao	gaol
	au	gauge
	ei	vein
	ey	they, prey
	é(e)	café, fiancée
b	b	book, rub
	bb	babble, flabby
ch	ch	church, cheese
	tch	match, watch
	t	question, future
	c	cello
	cz	Czech
d	d	dry, body, cold
	dd	cuddle, add
	ed	called
	ld	could, would, should
e	e	bed, better, berry
	ea	bread, instead, pleasure
	ai	said
	ay	says
	a	many, any
	eo	leopard
	ei	leisure
	ie	friend
	ae	aesthetic
ee	ee	sheep
	ea	team, please
	e-e	scene, mere
	e	equal
	ie	field, fierce
	ei	weird, ceiling
	ey	key
	eo	people

	oe	phoenix
	i	police, souvenir
	ay	quay
	ae	Caesar
eye	ie	pie, fiery
	i-e	bite, fire
	(e)igh	fight, height
	y	try, buy, dye
	i	island
	ai	aisle
f	f	finger, if, soft
	ff	off, sniff, coffee
	ph	physical, photograph
	gh	cough, enough
	lf	half, calf
	ft	often, soften
g	g	big, get
	gg	bigger, egg, aggravate
	gh	ghost, aghast
	gu	guard, guarantee
	x	example (pronounced -gz-)
h	h	hot
	wh	who
i	i	hit, infinite
	y	hymn, cylinder
	a	climate
	ie	sieve
	ei	foreign
	ai	mountain
	o	women
	u	busy, business
	e	English
j	j	judge
	dg(e)	judge, judg(e)ment

	g(e)	age, gem
	gg	exaggerate
	dj	adjust
	d	soldier, graduate
k	k	key, break
	c	can, panic, sceptic
	ck	back, cackle, panicky
	cc	tobacco, account
	q	quite, cheque
	ch	character, school
	cq	acquire, lacquer
	cch	saccharine
	lk	folk, talk
	kh	khaki
	x	extra (pronounced -*ks*-)
l	l	lead, spilt, bottle, medal
	ll	hell, calling, gorilla
m	m	me, mime, lump
	mm	common
	mn	solemn
	mb	bomb
	lm	calm
	gm	paradigm
	nm	government
n	n	not, sun
	nn	sunny
	kn	knot, knit
	gn	gnat
	pn	pneumonia
	mn	mnemonic
ng	ng	sing, longing
	ngue	tongue
	n	plank, sink
	nd	handkerchief

o	o	pot, rotten
	ou	cough
	a	watch, yacht
oh	o-e	wrote, owe
	oa	soap, load
	oe	toe
	oo	brooch
	ou	soul, though
	ow	grow
	ew	sew
	ol	folk, yolk
	eau	beau, plateau
	au	mauve
	eo	yeoman
oi	oy	boy, toy
	oi	poison
oo	oo	food, pool, troop
	u	truth
	ue	blue, true
	ou	group, through
	o-e	move, prove
	oe	shoe
	ew	crew, flew
	(o)eu	rheumatism, manoeuvre
	ui	fruit
ow	ow	now, power
	ou	our, plough, mouse
	au	sauerkraut
p	p	pin, sip
	pp	apple, nipped
	ph	shepherd
r	r	red, pretty
	rr	furry, purring
	wr	wrong, write

	rh	rhyme, rhythm
	rrh	diarrhoea, haemorrhage
s	s	sit, books
	ss	mess
	c	city, mice
	sc	scent, scene, fascinate
	ps	psychology
	st	fasten, castle
	sc	muscle
	sw	sword
sh	sh	sheep, fish, fashion
	ch	chivalry, machine
	s	sure, tension
	ss	mission
	sc	fascist, conscience
	c	ocean, special
	t	attention
t	t	tin, not, spilt
	tt	better, kettle
	th	Thomas, thyme
	ed	walked
	pt	pterodactyl, receipt
	bt	doubt, debt
	ct	indict
	ght	taught
u	u	cut, button
	oo	blood
	ou	trouble, young
	o	son, come, tongue
v	v	van, sieve, shiver
	vv	navvy
	f	of
	ph	Stephen

FINDING A WORD YOU CANNOT SPELL

w	w	wet, worn
	u	quiet
	o	one, choir
	wh	when, whether
y	y	yet, youth
	j	hallelujah
	i	opinion
yoo	ew	ewe, few, view
	u(e)	use, queue, cue
	eu	feud, pseudo
	eau	beauty
	you	youth
z	z	zero
	zz	puzzle, fizzy
	ss	scissors
	s	frogs, was, cheese
	x	xylophone
zh	s	pleasure
	z	seizure, azure
	ge	rouge

Remember the silent *h* at the beginning of words such as *hour* and *honour*. If you cannot find a word that begins with a vowel sound, try under *h*.